A Short History of New Brunswick

Dr. Ed Whitcomb

From Sea to Sea Enterprises

Ottawa

Library and Archives Canada Cataloguing in Publication

Whitcomb, Dr. Edward A.
A Short History of New Brunswick / Ed Whitcomb.

Includes bibliographical references and index.
ISBN 978-0-9865967-0-4

1. New Brunswick – History. I. Title.

FC2461.   W45 2010 971.5'1 C2010-902378-1

Printed in Canada by Dollco Printing, Ottawa

Table of Contents

This Book is Dedicated to the

People of

New Brunswick

Preface

This is the seventh in a series of history books on Canada's ten provinces. The idea for this series first arose in 1969 when I moved to Nova Scotia. Being new to the province and knowing very little about it, I went looking for a short history book which would provide an outline of the development of my newly-adopted home. There was no such book. In fact, there were hardly any short histories of any of Canada's provinces. In 1975, I decided to write the sort of book I had been looking for, and began with my native province of Manitoba. Over 8,000 copies of that *Short History of Manitoba* have been sold, which suggests that I was not alone in wanting good, short provincial histories.

The project to write histories of all the provinces was delayed by family and career, but the Centennials of Alberta and Saskatchewan put the series back on track, and the short histories of those provinces were published in 2005. It made sense to continue with western and then central Canada so *British Columbia* was published in 2006, *Ontario* in 2007, *Nova Scotia* in 2009, and *New Brunswick* and *PEI* this year. The series will be completed when *Newfoundland and Labrador*, *Quebec*, and *Northern Canada* are published in 2011-12.

A Short History of New Brunswick is designed to provide the average reader with a quick but accurate survey of the broad outline of the province's development. The emphasis is on the political developments that shaped the province as it is today, subjects such as the Natives, immigration and settlement, economic activities such as farming and fishing, and the attainment of Responsible Government. It explains the serious shortcomings of the Confederation arrangements, developments before World War I, prohibition, and the Depression. World War II and post-war developments complete the account.

Every historian has a point of view that determines which of the thousands of issues he or she will discuss, which of the millions of facts he or she will mention, and what things he or she will emphasize or ignore. This is essentially a political history, with some reference to economic, constitutional, military, and social developments, and it clearly emphasizes provincial rather than national or local issues. It seeks to explain New Brunswick's side in disputes between the province and the federal government. It is not popular history, and does not include pictures. While the achievements of New Brunswickers are documented, some criticisms are made of the heroes, politicians and groups who have shaped the province. In short, it is but one perspective on a very fascinating and complex society. My greatest hope is that this small book will encourage others to read more and to write more on the dozens of issues and perspectives necessary to obtain a full understanding of any society's development.

This account ends with the government of Richard Hatfield. Some readers would wish that it covered more recent developments, but there is a point where history merges into political science or journalism. While we know the broad outline of recent events, we do not have access to Cabinet decisions, correspondence, or the memoirs of most participants, and the secondary literature becomes less comprehensive. Many issues are still current, some still the subject of sharp debate, and many views on them are more subjective than objective. Much research has to be done and many books and articles written before the recent past falls into a proper historical perspective.

Many people helped with the preparation of this book. A number of professors, editors, analysts, and experts read part or most of the text, and made many valuable corrections and suggestions. They include Dr. William Acheson, Dr. Jerry Bannister, Dr. Maurice Basque, Dr. Gail Campbell, Dr. Don Desserud, Dr. Gerald Friesen, Margaret Poetschke, Robert Poetschke, Dr. John Reid, and Dr. Marc Robichaud. The cover design and map were prepared by Linda Turenne using a Natural Resources Canada map and the colours of the official flag of New Brunswick. Clifford Ford did the formatting and page layouts. John Colyer of Dollco Printers helped with the technical details. Most helpful of all was my wife, Kai, whose support and patience makes these books possible. I alone am responsible for the weaknesses that remain in the book.

Ottawa, May 2010.

Chapter 1

Beginnings to 1763

As with all territories, the history of New Brunswick is the product of the people who lived there and the land they inhabited. Geography dictated who their neighbours would be, their place on world trade and immigration routes, their natural resources, and the location of cities, towns and transportation routes. Geography affected politics, culture, religion, warfare and economic developments. Since the first contact with Europeans, New Brunswickers have earned their livelihoods primarily in forestry, fishing, and agriculture, economic sectors too often characterized by instability and low incomes. Contact with other provinces and the United States was difficult, which meant that that major wars were fought around the province rather than in it but also that major transportation routes pass it by. Before the province was established in 1784, it was part of the British colony of Nova Scotia, the French colony of Acadia, and the lands of the Natives.

New Brunswick is part of the Appalachian mountain chain that runs along the east coast of North America. Roughly square in shape, it is 320 kilometres from north to south and 240 kilometres from east to west, a total of 73,000 square kilometres. It is Canada's third smallest province. It can perhaps be subdivided into one huge region and four identifiable sub-regions. Almost 85% of New Brunswick consists of low mountains or hills, an area based on granite bedrock, heavily scarred by glaciers that ground the mountains from northeast to southwest. It is rugged and poorly drained, a land of forests and lakes. At 820 metres Mount Carleton in the northwest is the highest point in the province. This region is pierced by a number of major rivers which allow access to the rich timber resources, particularly the St. John in the south and west, the Miramichi which drains much of the northeast, and the Restigouche at the head of the Bay of Chaleur.

One sub-region is the southeast or the South Shore where the Bay of Fundy washes a rugged coastline of low mountains which face northwest. There are few good harbours except Saint John, where a small waterfall becomes the famous Reversing Falls when the world's highest tides rush upriver from the Bay of Fundy. Another geographic sub-region is the North Shore, the region facing the Bay of Chaleur, the Gulf of St. Lawrence, and the Strait of Northumberland. This region is part of the Gulf of St. Lawrence Plain, with patches of agricultural land along the shore and rivers. A number of villages gradually developed into towns and cities, including Campbellton, Dalhousie, Bathurst, Caraquet, Shippagan, Richibucto, Bouctouche and Shediac. The former towns of Newcastle and Chatham now form the City of Miramichi. Moncton lies on the Petitcodiac River which flows into the Bay of Fundy and marks a rough division between the South and North Shore regions.

The St. John River Valley contains much of the province's agricultural land, and is particularly suited for growing potatoes. The river is easily navigable past Fredericton, and is connected to an extensive river and lake system extending to within 100 kilometres of the St. Lawrence River. Major tributaries include the Oromocto, Kennebecasis, Tobique, Madawaska, and Nashwaak. The St. John is the largest river in the Maritimes and hosts major centres such as Saint John, Fredericton, Woodstock, Grand Falls, and Edmundston. Three hydroelectric dams on the St. John, Mactaquac, Grand Falls, and Beechwood, and another on the Tobique, provide much of the province's hydroelectric power. The fourth sub-region is the St. Croix Highlands, a rough triangle between Saint John, Fredericton, and St. Stephen. It is characterized by low hills, numerous rivers and bays, islands such as Grand Manan and Campobello, and fishing ports such as Blacks Harbour, St. Steven and St. Andrews.

New Brunswick was discovered, explored, and settled by peoples who came from Asia over 10,000 years ago. The Mi'kmaq, who lived in the northeast part of the province, were a semi-nomadic people, hunting moose, caribou, and beaver during the winter, and migrating to the coast in summer to fish for salmon, cod, seals, and whales, to hunt ducks and geese, and to gather oysters and clams. The Maliseet lived in the southwest and survived on agriculture, hunting, and fishing. The Passamaquoddy lived near the present-day border with Maine. These Natives mastered the rugged geography and inhospitable climate with birch bark canoes, snow shoes, fur clothes, and implements made of wood, clay, stone, and bone.

The Natives had well-established social organizations, assembling in large numbers in the summer while dispersing into smaller groups in winter. They believed that spirits lived in all objects, be they humans, animals, trees, or rocks. They had family units, but marriage was not necessarily permanent, and polygamy was practiced. In the centuries of warfare between the English and the French, the Natives allied with the latter. When France lost, the Mi'kmaq and Maliseet had to make peace with the English. Outnumbered and overwhelmed, they were devastated by disease, slowly relegated to dozens of small, uneconomic reserves, their land sometimes taken by Europeans, and eventually left in poverty by governments that violated the spirit if not the letter of their treaties.

In the late fifteenth century hundreds of fishing boats crossed the Atlantic every year and traded with the Natives. Jacques Cartier explored the northern coastline of New Brunswick in his famous 1534 voyage to the Gulf of St. Lawrence, and claimed the entire region of the present-day Maritimes for France. The land became known as L'Acadie, Acadia in English, a name of unclear origins. In 1604, Pierre du Gua, Sieur de Mons and Samuel de Champlain brought colonists to establish a base near the mouth of the St. Croix River. Because of the danger of attack by the Passamaquoddy Natives, De Mons built his settlement on Dochet Island. He seriously underestimated both the difficulty of bringing water from the mainland and the severity and length of the winter. Thirty-five of the seventy-nine men died, and the survivors went back to France or moved across the Bay of Fundy to found Port Royal. Over the next century, the population remained overwhelmingly Native, but one of the major successes of the French was converting them to Christianity, and relations between French and Natives were cordial and mutually advantageous.

The French or Acadian settlements expanded rapidly due to a low mortality rate and extremely high marriage and birth rates. In 1645, Nicolas Denys became possibly the first white settler in New Brunswick when he established a settlement at Nepisiquit on the Bay of Chaleur. Some groups crossed the Bay of Fundy to establish small settlements at Shepody and along the St. John River. After 1672, France granted huge estates to noblemen on the condition that they bring out settlers, but these efforts failed. In 1674, a Dutch sea captain, Jurriaen Aernoutsz, sailed from New Amsterdam (New York), and defeated the French on the St. Croix and St. John Rivers. He renamed the region New Holland, but the French soon re-conquered it. They then built forts at the mouth of the St. John, at Jemseg, and at St. Joseph (opposite Fredericton), trading posts which were repeatedly over-run by New Englanders, re-conquered by the French, abandoned and rebuilt.

In the 1630s, Charles de la Tour established a fur trading post near the mouth of the St. John River. This was a challenge to the Governor at Port Royal, Charles de Menou d'Aulnay. Both leaders were partners in the Company of New France, which had the fur trading monopoly, and their legal battles were taken as high as the royal court in Paris. De la Tour was ordered to hand the fort over to d'Aulnay. Instead, he went to Boston, hired some men, and attacked Port Royal. In 1645, d'Aulnay sent an expedition to capture his fort. La Tour was in Boston again, but his wife, Françoise-Marie Jacquelin, led a spirited defence of the garrison. It was hopeless, and following the surrender, she watched as her colleagues were hanged. Three weeks later she died. Shortly thereafter, d'Aulnay also died. De la Tour replaced his hated rival as Governor and married the widow, putting a dramatic and romantic end to the civil war.

New Englanders repeatedly attacked French posts in New Brunswick. In 1659, Colonel Thomas Temple captured the French posts on the St. John and built a fort at Jemseg, but the region was returned to France in the peace treaty of 1667. During these wars, the Natives usually found it advantageous to support the French. While successive peace treaties confirmed France's legal sovereignty, its actual control was tenuous. British victory in the War of the Spanish Succession (Queen Anne's War, 1701-1713) transferred sovereignty over part of Acadia from France to Britain. It was renamed Nova Scotia, but France retained Cape Breton Island. The borders of Acadia were far from clear, and France soon claimed that the land it had surrendered did not include the north shore of the Bay of Fundy or the Northumberland coast.

French strategy for preserving its North American possessions centered on the construction of a massive fortress at Louisbourg on Cape Breton Island. The Isthmus of Chignecto and the Northumberland coast formed a ring of defence for Cape Breton, and Acadians remaining under French authority were expected to provide supplies and militia The final contest for empire between Britain and France was fought out in the War of Austrian Succession, 1744-1748, and the Seven Years' War, 1756-63. The first war proved inconclusive, and the French then built Fort Beauséjour near the Missaguash River, just east of the present border with Nova Scotia, and Fort Gaspereau at the mouth of the Gaspereau River 17 kilometres northwest of Beauséjour.

The French strategic position in North America was very strong, and the British strategy was to bring massive superiority to bear on each point in its defences. In the spring of 1755, Britain sent 2,000 colonial militia and 500 regulars under Lieutenant Colonel Robert Monckton to face the 200 French regulars, Acadian militia and Mi'kmaq in Fort Beauséjour. The British attacked on June 13, and three days later the fort capitulated. Lieutenant Governor Lawrence was furious with the fact that hundreds of Acadians had been fighting for France. After the fall of Beauséjour, some Acadians engaged in guerrilla war. One group led by Joseph Broussard harassed the British in the Petitcodiac valley. Another under the skilled Canadian officer Charles Deschamps de Boishébert organized Acadians, Mi'kmaq, and Maliseet and defeated a force of New Englanders on the Petitcodiac River. From the St. John Valley to the Bay of Chaleur, Boishébert carried on guerrilla war so effectively that the British were often confined to their forts.

The Acadians wanted to remain neutral in the wars between France and England. Britain lacked the power to govern them, and it tried repeatedly to make them swear an oath of allegiance to the British crown. In July, 1755, Lieutenant Governor Lawrence ordered them to sign an unconditional oath or else. When they again refused, Lawrence concluded that they had deliberately opted for France. In 1755 he sent Lieutenant Colonel John Winslow to begin deporting them. Most were deported, but perhaps a third fled into the unpopulated areas of present-day New Brunswick, the Northumberland shore, Prince Edward Island, Cape Breton, and the interior of Nova Scotia.

The early years of the war went well for France, and Britain felt compelled to eliminate the Acadian threat. In 1758, Lieutenant Colonel Robert Monckton led a force of British regulars and New England Rangers up the St. John. The Rangers saw Acadians as military enemies, as French and Catholic, as allies of the Natives, and as occupiers of rich land. Their assaults on Acadian communities were vicious. Men, women, and children were killed, houses, barns, and churches burned, livestock killed, and crops destroyed. A few Acadians fled farther into the wilderness. The scene was repeated along the Northumberland coast, where General James Wolfe led a force which ruthlessly destroyed Acadian communities. The Maliseet made peace, but the Mi'kmaq continued to harass British forces and settlers for years. In the spring of 1760, France sent a fleet of ships to reinforce its position in New France. Unable to get past the British fleet on the St. Lawrence, it sailed to the head of the Bay of Chaleur. In June, the British caught up to it. The French scuttled one of their ships to avoid capture, and the British sank the other two. The 150 year struggle for supremacy in the Maritimes ended with the complete defeat of France.

British supremacy was confirmed at the Treaty of Paris of 1763, which transferred the whole of New France and the rest of Acadia to Britain. Nova Scotia now stretched from the St. Croix to the Madawaska, and the whole area was governed from Halifax. It was not clear where the border lay between that colony and the Thirteen American Colonies. Britain inherited France's claim that the border should be the Penobscot River. However, Britain's main goal after accepting American independence was to wean the United States from its alliance with France, and Britain therefore accepted the American demand that the border be the St. Croix River.

Chapter 2

A Province Is Born, 1763-1800

Before 1760, scarcely any European settlements took root in New Brunswick, with the exception of several small Acadian communities in the southeast. Permanent and peaceful settlement came as a result of Britain's victory over France and the American War of Independence. The first of the new permanent settlements was made by Acadians. New Englanders wanted to continue the deportations until the entire area was available for them to settle. The Acadians, however, no longer posed any threat. and they were excellent farmers, essentially self-governing, and uninterested in issues beyond their villages. With the approval of the authorities, Acadians began settling in large numbers in the Petitcodiac Valley and along the Northumberland coast in such communities as Shediac, Bouctouche, Shippagan, and Caraquet. Memramcook, at the south end of this region and Caraquet at the north became the centres of the Acadian community. Some Acadians returned to the St. John valley, but they were soon pushed upriver and eventually settled in the Madawaska region.

The Acadians survived the Deportation and the British attempt at assimilation failed. It was, indeed, counter-productive, because surviving the "Grand Deportation" became the central unifying theme in the Acadian identity. They remained a nation with a common identity based on ethnicity, culture, language, and history, an identity separate from that of their sister nation, the French Canadians of Quebec. In effect, the Seven Years' War transferred the heartland of Acadia from the Fundy shore of Nova Scotia to the Northumberland coast of what would soon become New Brunswick. Their challenge remained "survival," but the enemy was now the poverty of the soil to which they clung. A second challenge was that they soon became a small minority in an English-speaking Protestant province.

At the same time, New Englanders known as Planters began arriving to claim the land they felt they had conquered for Britain and especially for themselves. While most of them settled in the Annapolis Valley, some came to the Isthmus of Chignecto and the St. John Valley. Many of them were Congregationalists who later became Methodists and Baptists. These immigrants were successful at farming, fishing, lumbering, and commerce, and had money and equipment. Merchants occupied the site of Saint John and created a prosperous port. Planters settled on the good agricultural land running upriver from Saint John, where small communities emerged at Maugerville and

Gagetown. These settlers soon began tapping the resources of the region, and timber supplemented the fur trade which was still of some significance. Several other groups of settlers arrived including German Protestants, who settled on the Shepody and Petitcodiac Rivers, and English and Scots immigrants, who settled near Sackville. Farther north, two Scottish merchants, William Davidson and John Cort, obtained huge grants of land along the Miramichi, and began building ships and exporting furs, fish and lumber.

The outbreak of the American War of Independence raised the question of whether the New Englanders would join the rebellion. The merchants of Saint John were pro-British, but a significant portion of the New England settlers were quite sympathetic to the rebellious colonies. In 1776, New England privateers burned the vacant Fort Frederick at the mouth of the St. John. Jonathan Eddy led a force of Americans up the St. John River where they were warmly welcomed. Eddy's forces attacked Fort Cumberland, the former Fort Beauséjour, but were easily dispersed when 400 troops arrived from Halifax. The authorities made the wise decision to pardon the settlers on the grounds that they had been coerced into helping the Americans. The British Navy soon gained complete control of the Bay of Fundy and the coast of Maine, ending any further unrest or threat. American defeats and British bribes convinced the Natives that neutrality was their best option, and for the first time they were not an important factor in warfare. Throughout the rest of the war, Saint John profited from British demand for supplies and from privateering or the capture and sale of American merchant ships and their cargoes.

The Treaty of Paris of 1783 did not affect the borders of the colony of Nova Scotia, but the achievement of American independence transformed the region forever. A significant portion of the American population had sympathized with Britain and fought on the British side. When Britain lost the war, many of these "Loyalists" became refugees. Some 15,000 of them came to the northwest side of the Bay of Fundy. While most were British in origin, some were German, Dutch or Irish, and several hundred were Blacks. They came from all classes, all trades, and all professions. Most were destitute, and they needed land, housing, food, implements, and supplies to help them survive the first difficult years.

In May, 1783, around 3,000 Loyalists arrived near the mouth of the St. John, soon to be followed by 1,000 at Passamaquoddy Bay and a smaller number at Chignecto. The main migration of 11,000 came to Saint John in September, and others came to various locations in 1784 and 1785. Governor John Parr and the British authorities had done almost no planning for the influx of refugees. Loyalist officers assumed that they would receive large grants of land, and senior officers assumed they would receive huge estates. Their plan was to create a model society based on the feudal structures of Europe, in which they would be landlords with tenants and hired hands working their fields. The mass of the Loyalist exodus, however, consisted of farmers and workers, and had no intention of working someone else's estate. The war that had united them was over; the issues that divided them now came to the fore. In addition, many came from coastal areas, had no experience of frontier living and were not prepared for the harsher climate.

Governor Parr had previously granted huge tracts of land to the rich and powerful in Halifax and London. They were supposed to bring out settlers and to forfeit the land if they failed. No settlers had arrived, but Parr was reluctant to rescind their land grants. That confusion, the general lack of preparations, and the lateness in the season meant that most Loyalists spent a miserable winter in tent camps where food was inadequate, conditions were terrible, rumours of favouritism were rife, jealousy and suspicion abounded, and many people died. Governor Parr finally seized vacant land and made arrangements to allocate grants of 5,000 acres to the high-ranking officers. The British government vetoed that scheme – officers would receive 1,000 acres, others would receive 200. Loyalists began settling the land, cutting trees, building log houses and preparing to farm. At St. Andrews and St. Stephen, however, lots were surveyed and allocated by a fair draw before the settlers arrived, and settlement proceeded quietly and effectively.

The dream of creating an aristocratic society died at birth. The army officers who received grants of 1,000 acres discovered that they had to work the land themselves, and their status gradually declined towards that of the average farmer. Another dream that died at birth was that of the Blacks who believed that by supporting the British they could dramatically improve their lives. Most were freemen, and slavery soon became unfashionable, then unacceptable, and finally illegal by 1830. But they were given poor land and discriminated against, and many soon left for the free colony of Sierra Leone in Africa.

Before they had even left New York, the Loyalist leaders decided to create a separate province. They resented the role Halifax had played in the war, growing rich supplying the British forces while they had lost lives and property, and they did not intend to be governed by General Parr and his clique of friends. The lack of preparation for their arrival, the chaos of that first winter, and the problems with land grants added mightily to their argument. So did their numbers – 15,000 – and the difficulty of governing from far-away Halifax. On June 18, 1784, the British Government created a separate province, named after the German house of Brunswick.

The new Lieutenant Governor, Colonel Thomas Carleton, arrived that November. Carleton was a distinguished officer, but he failed to make the transition to Governor. He expected obedience from civilians, and found it difficult to make the compromises that politics required. He brought with him the new government consisting of Loyalists who had gone to London to lobby for jobs hoping to make their fortunes from those positions. The only local citizen appointed to that government was William Hazen, who represented the businessmen of Saint John. One of Carleton's first challenges was to create some form of local government for Saint John. He made it a city, the first incorporated city in British North America, with a government consisting of an appointed mayor assisted by six elected councilors.

Another question that had to be decided quickly was the location of the capital. Saint John was by far the largest community, the business and commercial capital, and the main port. But Carleton wanted a capital which would be free of the immediate influences of Saint John and its merchants. He wanted New Brunswick to be an aristocratic society dominated by landlords, with an economy based on agriculture rather than trade. He selected Fredericton, named for King George III's second son. It was closer to the centre of agricultural land, free from the danger of American attack, and within a short march of Saint John.

New Brunswick was created as a crown colony. All power rested with the Crown, that is, the government of England. It delegated authority to Lieutenant Governor Carleton, and he exercised that power through half a dozen officials called the Executive Council. They in turn governed the province through appointed magistrates selected largely from amongst the important Loyalists. This administration received most of its income from the British government, customs collected on imports, and from the sale or rent of land, all of which belonged to the crown. The members of the Executive also constituted the Legislative Council when they acted as an advisory body.

Carleton was instructed to establish a legislative assembly, and he called for elections in October-November 1785 to select 26 Members of the Legislative Assembly or MLAs. The franchise was quite wide for the period, with all men over 21 with three months residence entitled to vote, with the exception of Natives, Blacks and Catholics. There was stiff competition for the six seats in St. John County, violence erupted, and troops had to be called out. Elsewhere the election was more peaceful and the result favourable to Carleton's predispositions. The newly-elected Assembly was expected to approve the government's decisions, but it could influence and modify those decisions. It also had its own sources of revenue, which it could spend as it wished. In June, 1786, the first Assembly met in Saint John. It adopted all Nova Scotia laws and approved all the measures already taken by Carleton.

Within a decade the foundations of the colony of New Brunswick had been laid and decisions taken that would affect the province forever. Making it a viable political, economic, and cultural entity would take longer. The Governor and Assembly soon clashed over revenue and expenditure. Carleton could veto a budget, but not the individual items in it. The Assembly then passed a single budget which included items Carleton did not want. He then blocked the entire budget, and for four years little money was collected or spent, creating a serious gap in infrastructure that retarded economic development. Disagreements such as this continued for half a century.

This new government rested lightly on the population. From the beginning, people exhibited some disdain for the law. That attitude developed from the failure of the authorities to provide for an orderly settlement of land, to provide surveys and land titles, and to provide fair laws and proper law enforcement. It also resulted from the scramble for resources in which a few Loyalists used their power and influence to obtain land and positions, to make laws that favoured themselves, and to control the judiciary for their own benefit. Loyalists squatted on land to which they had no titles, and drove Natives and Acadians off their land. They cut timber on crown lands, and grazed cattle on public fields. Trees were dumped in rivers to float downstream and become someone else's problem. Nets were put across the mouths of streams to the detriment of the people up river, and people fished wherever they wanted. Smuggling became a normal economic activity for both rich and poor.

Despite these initial problems, New Brunswick emerged in a few years as a functioning society. All the Loyalists who wanted land received it as some 1,300,000 acres were granted to them. For several years there was considerable turnover of land titles as people searched for their ideal plot of land. Crops were planted and small surpluses became available to exchange for the goods every farmer needed. Small communities emerged, with a few stores and perhaps a church. Saint John grew as the entrepôt for timber exports and the import of almost every product the people needed or wanted. Carleton's small government began to provide rudimentary administration of customs and roads, and to pass and implement laws. Eight counties were marked out along St. John River, the Bay of Fundy and the Northumberland Strait. Almost all transportation was by sea or river, but a road was built from Saint John to Fredericton in 1793.

One element of the Loyalist dream came true, namely the creation of an established church, the Church of England, or Anglican Church. Both the Loyalist officers and the British government believed that weak religious principles were one of the underlying causes of the American revolt, and were determined to provide better moral leadership in the remaining British colonies. The

Anglican Church was given a privileged position in society and government, and its salaries, buildings, and expenses were subsidized. Anglicans, however, were never a majority, and favouritism towards the Church of England caused serious religious, social, political, legal, and educational problems. Marriage, for example, became a contentious issue. Anglican, Catholic, Presbyterian and Quaker ministers and justices of the peace could perform legal marriages, but not Methodists or Baptists.

During this period the southern portion of the border with the United States was agreed. The Treaty of Paris confirmed the St. Croix River as the border, but it was not clear which of the three rivers flowing into Passamaquoddy Bay was the St. Croix. Britain sent a team to find the site of De Mons's 1604 settlement at the mouth of the St. Croix River. They found the remains on Dorchet Island, which was at the mouth of the river farthest west, a British victory. That river, however, had two branches, and the commission agreed that the main one was the northern branch, a victory for the Americans. A cairn called The Monument was erected to mark its origin, approximately 90 kilometres west of Fredericton. It was also agreed that the major islands in Passamaquoddy Bay were British, including Grand Manan and Campobello. The border was not very important, however, because people moved freely over it, owned property on both sides, used the islands as they wished, and smuggled goods when governments attempted to prevent or tax trade.

The economy grew slowly as the initial influx of Loyalists settled down and began to produce food and timber. They quickly found that there were major restraints to economic growth. One was that it was very difficult to develop agricultural land, so effort was concentrated on the much more lucrative timber industry. Another was a severe scarcity of labour. A third was British land policy. After the Loyalists claims had been satisfied, London ordered that land could be sold but not granted. Land was the Crown's main asset, and it was assumed that potential buyers were available. In fact, immigrants could obtain free land in the United States, and land remained unsold to the detriment of immigration, timber production, agriculture, commerce, and government revenues. Carleton repeatedly demanded that the policy be abandoned, but London ignored his pleas.

British policy was also an impediment to the exploitation of New Brunswick's greatest resource, timber. The Baltic area of northern Europe was the main source of masts and wood for the British navy. When war erupted with France in 1793, Britain began obtaining masts from New Brunswick. Strict controls were imposed to reserve pine trees for the Navy, and were enforced by the Surveyor General. Britain, however, was in desperate need of every type of tim-

ber. A few surveyors could not control the forests, and merchants and lumbermen began cutting trees illegally, timber that easily found its way onto the
British market.

The outbreak of war between Britain and France in 1793 produced economic stagnation in New Brunswick. Britain's Caribbean colonies had to be
adequately supplied with food. Only the United States could meet that demand,
so American ships were given access to the West Indian trade. The Maritimes
could not compete, and small vessels then smuggled New Brunswick's products
out to American ships on the high seas, and traded for American goods which
were smuggled back into New Brunswick ports. Americans were also given
access to the inshore fishery, and fishermen moved to New England to work for
American fishing companies. Shipping, ship-building, fishing, agriculture, and
forestry all languished, and the population probably declined in the 1790s.

The war had other negative consequences. Troops were transferred to
Halifax, the colony losing the income produced by their expenditures. Authority
over the military was also transferred to Halifax. These were bitter personal
blows for Governor Carleton, who still fancied himself an important military
figure. To staff the vacated barracks, he recruited militia, which cost money and
further depleted the limited supply of labour. He sent the bills for the militia and
some repairs to fortifications to the Assembly, which rejected them on the
grounds that defence was an imperial responsibility. This incident added to the
growing tensions between Governor and Assembly as they constantly bickered
over expenditures. Finally, in 1803, he left for England after two decades as
Governor, his failures probably outweighing his triumphs.

Chapter 3

Growth, Prosperity and the Timber Trade, 1800-1835

The Napoleonic Wars brought prosperity and growth to New Brunswick for the first time. When war broke out again in 1803, France was able to restrict British access to timber from the Baltic region. Soon New Brunswick was supplying a quarter of Britain's needs. After 1807, French military victories effectively ended the export of Baltic timber to England. Britain could not be dependent on an unreliable source of timber no matter how cheap, and the decision was taken to make a permanent investment in New Brunswick and Canada. A tariff of 100% was placed on European timber for the duration of the war and into the immediate post-war period. British companies then made the investments necessary to supply Britain with New Brunswick timber. Local merchants who had struggled for two decades suddenly had more orders than they could fill. British companies arrived to help. Hundreds and later thousands of men were hired to cut trees. The logs were squared to reduce weight and to fit into ships, floated down river and collected at the ports. The supply of ships was inadequate, so ship-building companies flourished.

From 1807 to 1813, timber exports increased 600%. By 1810, much of the best timber had been taken out of the St. John Valley, and attention turned to the Miramichi where English merchants ran companies staffed with Irish and French workers. The Madawaska region also developed in this period. It was settled by Acadians moving up the St. John River and French Canadians coming south from the St. Lawrence Valley. Britain also decided to end its dependence on Americans to supply the West Indian market. It excluded foreign fish and subsidized fish from the Maritimes, measures which immediately revitalized the fishery. That added to the demand for ships for fishing and for transporting the fish to the West Indies. Fishermen who had emigrated to New England now returned to the booming ports along New Brunswick's coastline. Britain also relaxed rules designed to favour British over colonial ships in the cross-Atlantic trade, and New Brunswickers entered the European shipping business.

The outbreak of war with the United States in 1812 added to the economic boom. The war was mainly an attempt by the United States to conquer Upper Canada, and New Brunswick was not threatened by the fighting. It did, however, raise a regiment of troops which marched overland to Quebec, and participated in some of the major battles along the Niagara River. The war at sea began dismally for the British with a series of engagements won by American ships. British naval superiority was, however, quickly re-established, and neither American naval vessels nor privateers posed much of a threat after that. The war produced an enormous increase in spending by the British Government and its sailors and soldiers. Another source of prosperity was the sale of American ships and cargoes captured by the Royal Navy and by local privateers. Paradoxically, the war also stimulated trade with the United States. New England was opposed to the war, and the American government could not stop it from trading with the Maritimes.

Normally, peace brought such prosperity to an end, but this time the boom continued. While the wartime demand did indeed diminish, the Industrial Revolution was in full swing in Britain, producing a massive demand for timber. Equally important, the British Government left in place the tariff preferences for New Brunswick timber as well as the privileged access to the West Indian market. The result was an economic boom that lasted for half a century, the Golden Age of New Brunswick's history. Population tripled from 25,000 in 1800 to 75,000 in 1825. Saint John grew into a respectable port of 12,000, soon to become the largest urban centre in the Maritimes, and the third largest in British North America.

The British Isles had surplus population - tenants seeking their own land, workers rendered unemployed by the Industrial Revolution, tradesmen, and paupers. Local authorities did as best they could to accommodate this massive inflow of humanity. Many of the workers were single men or had left their families in Great Britain, and many came from hard-drinking societies. The immigrants needed every type of service – housing, food, education, and entertainment, especially that found in taverns. The towns and cities boomed with a rough class of unskilled and skilled labour. Some immigrants wandered upriver until they found a decent potential farm, and started clearing it for seeding. There was no point in surveying land unless it was going to be settled, and settlers then resented paying fees for surveys and titles. Highways were properly surveyed but local trails followed the path of least resistance. Many of these immigrants came as groups, founded communities, and were joined by more immigrants from the same areas in the British Isles.

Immigration changed the ethnic and religious map of the province. These newcomers were mainly Irish, largely Protestant in the south and Catholic in the north, with the Protestants divided between Anglican and Presbyterian. The forefathers of the Protestant Irish had emigrated to Ireland from Scotland or England several centuries earlier, and their descendants brought to New Brunswick an anti-Catholic bias that was reciprocated by the Catholics. In the absence of government services, religious and ethnic societies often provided education, charity, and a sense of community. This filled many needs, but it also maintained and accentuated religion as a divisive force. Presbyterian immigrants from Scotland formed a smaller group, and there was a small trickle of immigration from England and the United States. These Protestant groups assimilated into the Loyalist mainstream in terms of attitudes to business, government and community. In the northeast, the Acadian population expanded rapidly on the basis of a very high birth rate. Acadians moved up the valleys, westward along the coast, and into the Madawaska region. They were largely self-governing, with tight-knit communities which valued hard work, honesty, mutual support and large families, all centered on the Catholic Church and a clergy largely drawn from Quebec.

During this period, the Loyalist dream of an established Anglican Church began to falter. The Anglican Church sent too few ministers to meet the religious needs of its congregations, though after 1830, Kings College produced clergy drawn from the local population. The clergy preferred to live in towns, and on the frontiers some Anglicans converted to the newer evangelical religions, the Methodists and Baptists. Immigration , however, helped maintain the proportion of Anglicans amongst the general population. At first, the poorer classes embraced the evangelical religions while the elite remained strongly Anglican, but by the 1830s many rich merchants were Methodist or Baptist. Gradually, the Anglican near-monopoly on marriage disappeared, and governments began supporting the construction of non-Anglican churches.

The Loyalists also faced problems dominating higher education. Governor Sir Howard Douglas believed that the province needed a non-denominational institution of higher learning, and obtained support from both the British Government and the Assembly. The Anglican Church, however, wanted a single college for the entire region and for Anglicans only, namely Kings College in Windsor, Nova Scotia. Non-Anglican MLAs had no intention of supporting such a college, and Governor Douglas argued that if attendance were reserved for Anglicans, non-Anglicans would go to the United States for higher education. A compromise was agreed by which the institution was open to everyone, but all the main administrators were Anglican and all students had to attend daily Anglican services. As such, King's College opened its doors in Fredericton on January 1, 1829.

By 1815, it was clear that the province's economy would be based on the timber industry. The forests produced enormous exports of timber and lumber, and a plethora of secondary jobs in sawmills, shipbuilding, shipping and floating the logs downstream, and in the towns and cities that grew to meet the needs of all those engaged in the logging business. One way or another, logging touched most of the province's population – workers, merchants, lawyers, politicians, bartenders, and prostitutes. Not surprisingly, the ownership, control and exploitation of the forests was the dominant issue in provincial politics, and in relations between the province and the British government. Britain wanted to increase the earnings from the empire it had conquered and reduce the costs of its vast colonial network. The first step in tightening control was to transfer the power to regulate crown lands from the Surveyor General in Halifax to Lieutenant Governor George Smyth in Fredericton. Smyth established a regime to licence timber cutting, to obtain deposits from companies that received those licences, to ensure that they cut no more than the amount of timber agreed, and to cut it in the places specified.

These new fees soon exceeded all other sources of revenue, and were directly controlled by the Lieutenant Governor and his Executive. That made him more independent of the Assembly than before. The Assembly strongly opposed the new measures, partly because they strengthened Smyth's position and partly because many MLAs now had to pay fees when their companies cut timber. Battles between Smyth and the Assembly grew more frequent and bitter, especially over appointments, salaries and budgets. The new rules also impinged on the power and interests of the Executive, and Smyth sometimes found himself battling with his own government. One positive result, however, was that Smyth and the Executive now had more revenues to invest in province-wide needs such as trunk roads.

In 1824, Smyth was replaced by Lieutenant Governor Sir Howard Douglas. At the same time Britain appointed Thomas Baillie to manage the forests. The new system and Baillie's appointment created significant political problems. He was very effective, and companies that had previously cut timber illegally found themselves having to pay for licences. Baillie set licence fees arbitrarily which led to suspicions of favouritism, but London soon ordered him to auction timber rights to maximize revenue. He preferred to deal with a few dominant merchants, such as Joseph Cunard on the Miramichi and Alex Rankin on the Restigouche. Cunard's commercial empire suffered a setback in 1825, however, when the Great Miramichi Fire destroyed 15,000 square kilometres of timber and the town of Newcastle, and took 160 lives. Baillie also had a large role in immigration. He granted huge tracts of land to companies that promised to bring out immigrants. The New Brunswick and Nova Scotia Land Company received 500,000 acres in York County and between the Miramichi and the St. John Valleys. The company did not make a profit on this enterprise, but it did bring s large number of settlers to these areas.

Lieutenant Governor Douglas managed to avoid problems with the Assembly by spending most of the revenue on projects he knew the MLAs favoured, and he was possibly the most popular governor in the province's history. His successor, Sir Archibald Campbell, was less astute. More people began to believe that crown lands should be controlled by the Assembly, where the timber merchants had considerable influence. The main battle over crown lands was joined when London decided that it wanted the Assembly to pay government salaries. That was not a financial problem for the province because those salaries were already being paid out of the timber licence fees. It was a problem for the Assembly, though, because it did not collect those fees. And if it paid officials' salaries, it would want a major say in appointing those officials, something the Lieutenant Governor and London had always controlled.

For years the two sides wrangled over how to implement the change. The appointment in 1835 of a new Colonial Secretary, Lord Glenelg, produced a more flexible attitude, particularly as Upper and Lower Canada were heading towards rebellion, and London wanted no trouble in the Maritimes. In 1837, control of the forests and timber licence fees was transferred to the Assembly. It then took responsibility for government salaries, and guaranteed the salary levels of all existing officials. It was agreed that when officials retired or died, their replacements would receive lower salaries. This arrangement represented a considerable transfer of power from London and the Lieutenant Governor to the Assembly. It solved many of the most important grievances of the province especially those between the Assembly and the Lieutenant Governor, to the considerable advantage of the former. Another problem that was gradually solved was that the forests that had been reserved for the British Navy were opened up to exploitation.

The magnitude of these changes was soon evident. The budget controlled by the Assembly more than doubled, from £83,000 in 1836 to £200,000 in 1840. In addition, it gained control of £153,000 that had been accumulated over the years. This flood of money allowed it to act as an alternate government, spending much of this revenue on transportation and education. The Assembly ended Baillie's practice of selling huge blocks of crown lands to rich merchants. In future, land could only be sold in lots of 100 acres for agriculture. The timber merchants were pleased with the change because they could obtain access to timber in return for small annual fees, without complicated conditions such as bringing out immigrants.

Chapter 4

Responsible Government and the Smashers, 1835-1860

The movement towards Assembly control of lands and responsibility for government salaries propelled the province towards Responsible Government, though neither provincial politicians nor the British Government fully understood the direction, the process, or the eventual outcome. With the Assembly controlling so much of overall spending, the Lieutenant Governor found it increasingly difficult to manage the province the way he wanted. Reformers in the Assembly led by Lemuel Allen Wilmot asked Colonial Secretary Glenelg to expand the Executive Council and appoint more members acceptable to the Assembly. Glenelg instructed Lieutenant Governor Archibald Campbell to do so, in order to achieve "harmony" between Assembly and Executive.

This would be an important step towards Responsible Government, and Campbell procrastinated because it would weaken his power. On September 10, 1836, Glenelg again ordered Campbell to appoint some members acceptable to the Assembly, to speed up the transfer of control over crown lands to the Assembly, and to make those instructions public. It became clear that Campbell had been disobeying instructions, and he was recalled in early 1837. His replacement, Sir John Harvey, dismissed one member of the Executive and appointed Charles Simonds, the Speaker of the Assembly, and three other new members who enjoyed support in the Assembly.

The movement towards Responsible Government gathered momentum due to the growing pressure in the colonies to exercise more control over local matters coupled with a growing desire in Britain to reduce the costs of maintaining the Empire. They were related - if the colonies were going to carry a greater share of the costs of Empire, then they had to be given a greater say in local government. The next stage in the process occurred when the Colonial Secretary, Lord John Russell, instructed Lieutenant Governor Harvey to appoint executive members "during pleasure" instead of during "good behavior." The latter, in effect, meant for life, while the former meant that the governor could dismiss these appointees if he so chose. That opened the way for the governor to dismiss the Executive if it was not in "harmony" with a majority of MLAs. The new rules applied only to future appointments, but the principle was accepted, and the practice of holding offices as pieces of property for life was ended.

Full Responsible Government finally came to New Brunswick following developments in Canada and Nova Scotia. The new Lieutenant Governor,

Sir William Colebrooke, accepted that his Executive had to have the confidence of the Assembly, but it was not yet established that it had to be composed of MLAs. Colebrooke saw himself as the leader of the Executive, and called an election in 1843 hoping that politicians who supported him would win. His opponents won, and Colebrooke dutifully replaced four of the five members of the Executive with officers more amenable to the Assembly.

On December 24, 1849, the position of provincial secretary became vacant, and Wilmot, the reform leader, proposed that an MLA should receive the appointment. Instead Colebrooke appointed his own son-in-law, an act that bordered on defiance of the new policy of the British Government. Wilmot and three others resigned from the Executive and took the issue to the Assembly. It approved motions stating that Colebrook's action was unacceptable and that the Executive did not have the confidence of the the Assembly. Colebrooke dismissed some more members of the Executive and replaced them with others acceptable to the Assembly. London vetoed the appointment of the son-in-law as provincial secretary, and Colebrooke then selected an MLA for the position. On 31 March 1847, the new Colonial Secretary, Lord Earl Grey, ordered the Lieutenant Governor of Nova Scotia to appoint an Executive drawn exclusively from the Assembly. That instruction applied equally to New Brunswick, and its Assembly gained effective control over local government.

The post-Napoleonic period of prosperity, stability, and economic and population growth came to a temporary end in the early 1840s. Britain abandoned preferential tariffs for New Brunswick timber which sent the economy into a serious depression. Companies went bankrupt and people emigrated to the United States. At the same time, famine in Ireland led thousands of poor and sick emigrants to sail for North America, many of them landing in New Brunswick where the authorities were hard pressed to deal with the influx. Nine thousand of them came in 1846, another 17,000 in 1847. Often they were transported in crowded, unsanitary ships. They brought disease, which forced the government to establish a quarantine base on Partridge Island in Saint John harbour where as many as 2,000 died. The immigrants crowded into slums, providing the towns and cities with a cheap source of labour. Many of them moved on to the United States but by 1851, over half of the province's population was Irish with a majority of them Catholic. In the decade the population increased from 190,000 to 250,000, but Protestants still outnumbered Catholics.

Conflicts between the two groups had started as early as 1838, and they quickly escalated in the late 1840s, especially in Saint John. One important factor was economic – poor, starving Irish Catholic immigrants needed whatever work they could obtain at whatever wage they were offered. That threatened the incomes of existing workers, many of whom were Protestant. Fear of disease and loss of political power were also serious concerns for the Protestants. The battles pitted Catholic against Protestant, but it was also ethnic because almost all Irish Protestants were the descendants of English Anglicans and Scottish Presbyterians. Both sides had their organizations, the most important being the secret Orange lodge which was dedicated to maintaining Protestant domination of society, politics and the economy. The conflict was, in short, primarily ethnic, and non-Irish Catholics and many Protestants were not directly involved.

The main Orange celebration was on July 12, the anniversary of the 1690 victory of King William of Orange that ensured British domination of Ireland. The "Glorious Twelfth" was celebrated by marches, and to assert their dominance, they deliberately marched through Catholic neighbourhoods. That prompted Irish Catholics to erect arches painted green in order to force the Orangemen to go "under the green," a symbolic gesture of subservience. Riots broke out at the sites of these arches. In 1847 several Catholics were killed in a very serious riot in Woodstock. An all-Protestant jury determined that the Catholics had started the riot, and found guilty 34 of the 39 Catholics who had been charged. Smaller riots took place in Saint John and Fredericton. On July 12, 1849, thousands of Orangemen descended on Saint John to demonstrate their power and to provoke the Irish Catholics in their neighbourhood of York Point. There the Catholics built an arch which the mayor himself attempted to remove. Police could not prevent rioting, and 60 soldiers had to be called out to restore order. The mayor was injured and a dozen men died in the most violent clash of the nineteenth century. This time both Protestants and Catholics were charged, but Protestants received lighter sentences.

During this period another stretch of the border with the United States was settled. The land border was to run north from the origins of the northern branch of the St. Croix to the watershed of the St. Lawrence. Unfortunately, no such watershed could be identified. The region of the upper St. John River Valley came into dispute between the state of Maine, New Brunswick, and Lower Canada. American claims included the east bank of the St. John, and if accepted, would have precluded a British-controlled transportation link between the lower St. John and Quebec. The United States and Britain agreed that the King of the Netherlands could arbitrate the dispute. He gave that part of the region to New Brunswick, but Maine rejected the proposal.

A decade later serous disputes again broke out between loggers. Lieutenant Governor Harvey sent two companies of soldiers to Woodstock and Grand Falls. The governor of Maine called up 10,000 militiamen, effectively starting the "Aroostook War." An American arbitrator and Harvey quickly put an end to the Aroostook War, a somewhat misnamed adventure since the only casualties occurred during a brawl in a tavern. The agreement provided for Britain to continue to administer the Madawaska and for the Americans to administer the Aroostook.

In 1842, London and Washington appointed negotiators with orders to compromise on the conflicting claims. Americans had never controlled the east side of the St. John River, so recognizing that territory as British was not a major problem to the American negotiator. The British saw controlling the Aroostook as desirable but not essential. The two negotiators therefore agreed on a border running north from the Monument that marked the headwaters of the St. Croix River to Grand Falls. From there it followed the St. John northwest almost to Edmundston, then 60 kilometres farther west creating a small rectangle between northeast Maine and Quebec. The only New Brunswick border still in dispute was that with Lower Canada. In 1851, arbitration gave New Brunswick over half of it, and in 1873, the region became the county of Madawaska.

Having attained Responsible Government, the province had to learn how to manage it. There were no precedents in British colonial experience, and each of the North American colonies stumbled forward into uncharted waters. It was not clear how much power Britain had devolved to the colonies, how much that of the lieutenant governors had devolved to the assemblies, how that power was divided between the elected assemblies and the appointed legislative councils, and how they all related to the executive council.

Lieutenant Governor Sir Edmund Walker Head had clear instructions to form an Executive drawn from the Assembly. In 1848, he kept the most prominent leaders from the existing government and added leaders from other major factions. The new provincial secretary (premier) was Edward Chandler, ably assisted by Robert Hazen representing the Saint John merchants, plus the leaders of the reformers, Charles Fisher and Lemuel Allan Wilmot. Head pressed for the Executive to be given the authority to propose projects important to the whole province, and gradually the power of the Executive increased. As the province became more interested in building railways, it discovered that the Executive could not borrow money abroad when the Assembly controlled spending including paying interest on the provincial debt. That forced the Assembly to pass the power to initiate spending to the Executive, with the Assembly retaining the power to approve or reject such proposals.

With Responsible Government in place, the Assembly began to exert more influence. It refused to contribute to improvements to military fortifications and it abolished the provincial militia, which had long been an annoyance because of the cost and inconvenience to merchants who lost their workers for a few days every year. The Assembly had taken over the civil list in return for control of crown lands, and gave London a fixed amount every year to pay official salaries. It soon began criticizing those salaries and the number of office holders, making slow but steady progress in reducing the number and salaries of officials. London retained the right to veto provincial legislation, and the reports of the Lieutenant Governors were important inputs into any such decisions. The Assembly therefore demanded to see those reports so they could rebut any arguments he made for vetoing their decisions.

The Chandler regime failed to implement these changes as rapidly as many MLAs wanted, and lost a vote in the Assembly. It resigned in May 1857, the first time Responsible Government was actually tested. The next Lieutenant Governor, John Thomas Manners-Sutton, called on the leading politicians who had brought down the government to form a new administration. They then won an election on a platform of "smashing" the remaining vestiges of colonialism. The Smashers set out to abolish the last privileges of the Anglican Church with considerable enthusiasm. The government strengthened the public-supported schools but its attempt to introduce a compulsory free non-denominational school system foundered on the fact that the enormous Irish and Acadian Catholic minority and many Anglicans opposed this idea.

One of the Smashers' favourite crusades, namely prohibition, ended in failure. In the 1840s, the Sons of Temperance grew rapidly in membership, organization and enthusiasm, as did other organizations dedicated to the moral improvement of mankind through the prohibition of alcohol. Excessive drinking was a serious problem, especially when lumbermen emerged from the camps in the spring and spent days drinking to excess and terrorizing towns and cities. On January 1, 1853, the Assembly passed a law prohibiting the import of liquor. The courts would not enforce the law, the mayor of Saint John continued to issue tavern licences, and the number of taverns in Moncton actually increased. Where taverns were closed, illegal drinking spots immediately opened. Government revenue fell by one-sixth, and the cost of enforcement mounted.

The leader of the Sons of Temperance was Samuel Leonard Tilley. In 1855, he introduced a law tightening up the loopholes in the previous legislation. It was approved by only 21 to 18 votes. While half the population was very pleased, the other half was outraged. Militant prohibitionists searched for violators and gave their names to the police. It proved impossible to enforce the legislation, and parts of the province descended into lawlessness and near revolt. Lieutenant Governor Manners-Sutton instructed the government either to enforce or change the legislation. When it failed to do either, he engineered its defeat and called an election. London was distressed with this violation of

Responsible Government, but the results bore him out. The election was fought between the Smashers and the Rummies, and when the latter won a clear victory, prohibition was repealed by a vote of 38 to 2.

The Rummies could not agree on other issues, however, so the Lieutenant Governor was forced to call another election. This time the Smashers won and proceeded with their plans to improve the people and province in ways other than legislating prohibition. They introduced the secret ballot, an important step towards full democracy which also reduced the amount of violence that had accompanied open voting at public meetings. They extended the franchise to include almost all white men. Their democratic enthusiasm had its limits – women had lost the vote in 1843, and the Smashers did nothing to reverse that measure.

The economy stagnated in the 1840s due to the termination of preferential access to the British market. Other markets had to be found, and all of Britain's North American colonies looked to the United States. The Treaty of Reciprocity of 1854 solved the problem. Raw materials from New Brunswick and the other colonies were allowed into the United States, and American fishermen gained legal access to the inshore fishery. New Brunswick benefitted since timber was its main export, and the fishery was not that important. Exports to the United States surged, more than replacing lost exports to Britain. That treaty also marked a significant milestone in de-colonialization as it had to be ratified by the Assembly, the first time this body had exercised any role in foreign affairs.

Soon the economy was booming once more. Hundreds of ships were built, loaded with exports, and both ship and cargo sold. The crews found their way home to man another ship that had been built to replace the one just sold. Some merchants set up major shipping companies, and New Brunswick became an important factor in global transportation. They were assisted by the fame gained by vessels such as the *Marco Polo*, which set a record for the return trip to Australia. The decade also marked the acceleration of industrialization with the establishment of iron foundries, ship building, fish processing and factories turning out textiles, leather products, furniture, machinery, soap, and metal products. Although the MLAs continued the practice of spending most revenue locally, they also built a network of provincial roads connecting the counties within the province itself, and connecting the province to Quebec and Nova Scotia.

While the Orange order fought to keep Catholics down, the Anglican Church saw its remaining privileges whittled away by the Baptists and Methodists who now dominated the Assembly. One privilege, the inclusion of an Anglican in the Legislative Council, required four years of political infighting to resolve. The status of King's College was also under attack. There was resentment over the fact that a large annual grant supported an underutilized faculty of theology and produced few students. In 1859, control of King's College was transferred from the Anglican Church to the government. In its place the non-denominational University of New Brunswick was established in 1859, with a governing senate of eight laymen, no religious tests for admission, and no faculty of theology. The Assembly granted support to a Baptist Seminary in Fredericton and to the Methodist school founded in Sackville by Charles Allison. The latter became Mount Allison University in 1858, and made history shortly after as the first university in the British Empire to grant a degree to a woman.

The 1850s also saw the beginning of railway construction, an issue that would dominate politics for decades, intensify regional rivalries, create fortunes, turn towns such as Moncton into cities, and eventually become one of the main factors leading to Confederation. The logical routes for railways formed a triangle around the periphery of the province, with each side competing for support. One route was along the southeast coast from Saint John to Shediac on the Northumberland Strait. If it could be connected to lines in Maine, it might become a major railway because Shediac was far closer to Europe than was Boston. Another potential route came down the St. John Valley from Quebec and then either south from Woodstock to St. Andrews or east through Fredericton to Saint John. Both of these proposed lines ran through populated areas, were commercially viable, and had powerful supporters, but there was insufficient money for two lines.

A third possible route ran from Quebec to Campbellton and along the coast to Nova Scotia and Halifax. That route could never be commercially viable, and its main justifications were military – to move troops quickly between colonies – and political – to unite the British colonies. It could only be built with massive government support from Britain. Saint John was totally opposed, because if Halifax were the terminus for a railway from central Canada, it would replace Saint John as the dominant Maritime port.

Against this backdrop of fractured geography, competing interests, and limited finances, New Brunswick embarked cautiously and fitfully on the age of railways. Britain was not interested in paying for a Quebec-Halifax line, and the first meaningful proposal came from the Americans for a railway from Bangor, Maine, to Halifax through Saint John, that is, the Saint John-Shediac line with southern and eastern extensions. It became known as the Europe and North American Railway, the E&NAR, and in 1850, the Assembly voted to support it as well as a line from St. Andrews to Quebec along the St. John Valley. Construction began, but both lines soon ran into cost overruns and missed deadlines. The viability of these projects was also thrown into question with the opening of a line from Montreal to Portland, Maine, which gave central Canada access to an ice-free port.

By the mid-1850s, the E&NAR had failed, and the New Brunswick government took control of it. It had not been completed to the American border, so it produced only a fraction of the revenue anticipated as part of a trunk line from Bangor to Shediac. The St. Andrews-Quebec line had been renamed the New Brunswick and Canada Railway and Land Company. By 1862, it stretched from St. Andrews to a point near Woodstock. It then went bankrupt, and the government had to operate it. Meanwhile, Nova Scotia built a line from Halifax to Truro and offered to extend it to New Brunswick if a line were built connecting this line to Shediac. New Brunswick rejected that proposal because Saint John wanted no competition from Halifax. In Canada, the Grand Trunk Railway had reached Rivière du Loup, but New Brunswick had no interest in a railway along its own north shore linking Halifax and Canada. The decade ended with the province owning bits and pieces of several railways that did not fit into any coherent overall strategy to link the colony to outside markets or to other colonies. The 1860s would change all that.

Chapter 5

Confederation, 1860-1867

As New Brunswickers celebrated New Years Day on January 1, 1860, they could hardly have expected that they were entering the most decisive decade of their history. New Brunswick was one of six British North American colonies north of the Caribbean. By 1867 it would be one of four provinces in a large, federal colony called Canada. The New Brunswick of 1860 was a prosperous, self-confident, independent-minded colony. It had enjoyed almost half a century of economic growth, its population expanding to 190,000 by 1851. Its voters were generally content with the their lives in this small corner of the British Empire.

Their world was changing, however, in terms of trade relationships, transportation networks, the structure of the British Empire, relations with other British North American colonies, and relations with the United States. It was far from clear where these cross-currents would lead. New Brunswick faced four options for the future, one being the maintenance of the status quo as a self-governing British colony. When Confederation was adopted years later both Prince Edward Island and Newfoundland opted to remain separate colonies. The people of Nova Scotia voted overwhelmingly against Confederation in 1867, the people of Red River rebelled and were conquered, and British Columbia demanded massive concessions before it agreed to join the new federation. Confederation, in short, was far from inevitable in 1860.

A second option was Maritime Union. It called for New Brunswick, Nova Scotia, and Prince Edward Island to join together in a single colony with one government and a much larger economic, demographic and political base. That meant, however, that all three provinces would lose their independence, at least two of the capital cities would lose their status, and most of the MLAs and ministers would lose their jobs. Had Confederation failed, however, Maritime Union might have succeeded. Another option was annexation to the United States. Since its founding, New Brunswickers had traded with New England. The Loyalists rejected American independence, but many of them were comfortable with American views on trade, economics, politics and society. Most Irish immigrants went to the United States, including many who settled first in New Brunswick, and Irishmen hardly regarded citizenship in the American Republic as a disadvantage.

In 1860, the idea of Confederation with the other British colonies faced serious obstacles. Nova Scotia was a rival, with a different demography and economy. New Brunswick shared few interests with Newfoundland, and viewed Canada in a generally unfavourable light. There was little trade between them and little prospect for more. And while Canadian politicians and businessmen looked to expansion to the Pacific, New Brunswickers looked to continued links across the Atlantic and to the south.

Railways played an important but not dominant role in the drama. Two railway schemes were important to the Confederation debate. Local interests favoured the old plan for a line connecting the north-eastern United States with Europe through the Saint John-Shediac route. Some Canadian, Nova Scotia and British interests favoured a route from Rivière-du-Loup to Campbellton and on to Halifax, the so-called Intercolonial Railway. In New Brunswick that route had little political support. Instead, in 1864, the Assembly passed an act which subsidized construction of branch lines from the Saint John-Shediac main line. Those branches ran in so many directions they looked like a lobster's claws, and the legislation became known as the Lobster Act.

In the early 1860s, Lieutenant Governor Arthur Hamilton Gordon began a campaign to promote Maritime Union. He convinced Provincial Secretary Leonard Tilley of its merits. The Provincial Secretary of Nova Scotia, Charles Tupper, agreed, but Prince Edward Island was not interested so the idea lay dormant. During this period, politics in Canada reached a stalemate, and Canadian leaders began looking elsewhere for solutions to their political, constitutional and economic problems. Hearing of proposals for a conference of Maritime politicians, they asked for an invitation. The three Maritime governments then decided to hold the conference, and scheduled it for Charlottetown beginning on September 1, 1864. The New Brunswick delegation consisted of Tilley, Edward Chandler from the opposition, and three other delegates.

At the conference the Canadians proposal for federal union of all British North American colonies quickly superseded the issue of Maritime Union. For the New Brunswick delegation, the wider union meant greater trade opportunities, outside support for the Intercolonial Railway, and continuation as a separate province albeit with lesser responsibilities. It was agreed that the new colony would have a strong federal government. While lavish dinner parties and vast quantities of liquor did much to facilitate compromise and agreement, in general these decisions appealed to the New Brunswick delegation.

In October, Tilley and six delegates left for a federal conference in Quebec City to work out the details of the Confederation scheme. There they do not seem to have made a major effort to defend their province's interests, or if they did, they were not very successful. Edward Chandler fought for greater powers for the provinces. John A. Macdonald, the leader of the Canadian delegation, thwarted that because he wanted to maximize the power of the central government. It was agreed that the House of Commons would be based on representation by population, which gave New Brunswick 16 of the 200 seats. On that basis it would have one or two seats at the cabinet table and a small voice in the affairs of the federation. One of the main goals of Confederation was to acquire and populate the prairies, so it was also clear that New Brunswick's small share of power in Ottawa would gradually decline.

To balance central Canada's overwhelming representation in the Commons, the Maritime provinces had to ensure that the Senate would share power with the Commons and that the smaller provinces would have strong representation in the Senate. The American Senate provided a model, because each state had the same number of Senators and they were appointed by the states and therefore represented the people of those states. Instead, the Maritime delegates accepted that each region would have 24 Senators. They also accepted that the Maritimes was a single region, and that Canada consisted of two regions, Upper and Lower Canada, even though it was a single colony and had sent only one delegation to the Charlottetown Conference. Ontario and Quebec thus obtained twice as many Senators as the three Maritime provinces combined. It was decided that Senators would be appointed by the central government and not by the provinces, and they would have much less power than American ones. In short, Tilley and his colleagues agreed to the creation of a federation in which New Brunswick would exercise a small and decreasing amount of power and in which the Maritimes would have no means of preventing the adoption of measures that could be very harmful to them.

The New Brunswick delegation does not seem to have had serious concerns with the transfer of responsibilities to the new federal government in Ottawa. New Brunswick MLAs had always regarded local matters as of more importance than regional concerns, and Confederation left them in control of local issues. The most important economic and political factor in New Brunswick was the forest, and natural resources or crown lands including forests remained a provincial responsibility. Inter-colonial railways became a federal responsibility, which meant that an inter-colonial railway would be built and Ottawa would pay. Fiscal and monetary policy came under the new central government, and Ottawa took over New Brunswick's debt. Fisheries went to Ottawa, a serious loss for Nova Scotia but not for New Brunswick. Tariffs or customs, which had accounted for more than half the revenues of the New Brunswick government, would be collected by the central government. As compensation, Ottawa was to provide a subsidy, but the New Brunswick delegation accepted an amount that did not come close to covering the responsibilities that the province retained.

Shortly after their return from Quebec, Tilley and the other delegates realized that they had seriously misread public opinion. New Brunswick's virtually powerless position in the new federation was grasped immediately by those who read the proposals. When the agreement was reported in the newspapers on November 7, 1864, a storm of protest erupted. Nova Scotians had the same reaction, and both Prince Edward Island and Newfoundland rejected Confederation. Tilley had to explain the advantages of an arrangement that a majority of people in the Maritimes and Newfoundland found wanting in very serious ways.

Tilley, the other delegates, and the pro-confederation MLAs and their supporters worked to obtain Assembly approval for the Quebec Resolutions. They spent their time and energy defending the agreement. They made no serious attempt to re-open negotiations and obtain terms acceptable to their people, even though the Maritime provinces were is a very strong bargaining position because Confederation could not proceed without their agreement. Tilley and other delegates said that the Intercolonial would terminate in Saint John and not Halifax, that taxes would not be increased, and that the Maritimes would have enough political strength to prevent the federal government from raising tariffs and spending money on transportation facilities elsewhere in Canada.

They could not, however, point to any proof of these assertions in the agreement. In fact, they were being less than truthful because the Intercolonial would indeed terminate in Halifax, tariffs were raised almost immediately, and Ottawa used money collected throughout Canada to buy the Northwest Territories, build canals in Ontario and Quebec and build a railway to British Columbia. The pro-Confederates said that New Brunswick's industries would gain access to the bigger central Canadian market, but the Saint John merchants were skeptical that they could compete with central Canadian industry even in New Brunswick. The pro-Confederate side used the threat of potential invasion by the United States to argue that Confederation would strengthen colonial defences. In fact, the threat did not exist, and Confederation was not needed to move troops between provinces.

Like Tupper in Nova Scotia, Tilley was afraid to submit the Quebec Resolutions to the Assembly. His government was divided on the issue. The second most powerful minister, Albert Smith, was vehemently opposed, and another minister resigned. For months Tilley and Lieutenant Governor Gordon discussed tactics, and Tilley finally agreed to Gordon's advocacy of an early election. It was called for February 1865. It was already too late, however, because most New Brunswickers rejected the agreement as soon as they understood the terms. The main newspapers came out against it. Irish Catholics opposed it because they saw Upper Canada as dominated by Orangemen, and Acadians had no interest in being an even smaller linguistic minority in a larger English-dominated federation. Tilley was criticized for calling a snap election before the issues had been properly debated. Another issue was skepticism about the worth of Canadian promises, based in part on their reneging on previous agreements to build the Intercolonial Railway. That led to demands that the promise to build the Intercolonial be written into any new constitution. Tilley begged Macdonald to agree but he refused, reinforcing the negative views of Canadian promises.

Smith and the Anti-Confederates won the election with 26 out of 41 seats, and every delegate to the Quebec Conference was defeated. But Smith's problems had just begun. The only thing that united his supporters was opposition to Confederation, and they opposed it for different reasons. Smith unfortunately lacked the qualities needed to hold the disparate coalition together. Opposing confederation was negative; Maritime Union had little support; and there were growing worries about a future as a separate colony. The only viable alternative to Confederation was therefore closer relations with the United States. That prospect depended on making progress on the old dream of a railway from Maine through Saint John to Shediac. The Saint John-Shediac line was complete, but a line called the Western Extension was needed to connect Saint John with the American border. The Americans made no effort to build an extension on their side of the border, and Smith could not obtain financing for the Western Extension in London. More seriously, in the spring of 1865, the Americans made it clear that they would not renew the Reciprocity Treaty, the arrangement that had sustained New Brunswick's prosperity after losing preferential access to the British market. Increased trade with Canada and Nova Scotia was a poor alternative, but it was now the only one.

With his railway and trade policies in ruins, Smith's coalition began to disintegrate. One minister resigned, and another decided to support Confederation. In a crucial by-election in Fredericton in November 1865, the pro-Confederation candidate, Charles Fisher, won by a substantial margin. He did so by appealing to Protestants and to loyalty to the crown. In addition, at Tilley's request, John A. Macdonald sent $5,000 which was more than enough to persuade the undecided. While the pro-Confederates were willing to bribe voters, Smith's scruples as a reformer made him reluctant to use even accepted levels of patronage to win his battles.

At this stage the actions and attitudes of the British government became significant factors. London was strongly in favour of Confederation. It would reduce the costs of administration and improve relations with the United States by allowing Britain to withdraw its troops. Its views, however, had not been made public. After Tilley lost the 1865 election, the British government decided to intervene. The Colonial Secretary, Edward Cardwell, telegraphed Gordon "to do all in his power to push it through." Gordon then published the correspondence which proved that the British government strongly supported Confederation. The province had rejected it in 1865 partly because it believed it would weaken ties with Britain. Now British views were clear, and it seemed unpatriotic to oppose the mother country's wishes.

The March 1866 Speech from the Throne scarcely mentioned Confederation, and it was not seriously debated. The government was facing a financial crisis, and Smith's position on Confederation began to soften. He began discussions with Gordon in case Confederation did emerge as the only option. Public opinion was also shifting as more people came to see Confederation as inevitable. On April 6, Gordon precipitated a crisis by arranging for the Legislative Council to send an address to the Queen supporting Confederation. That surprised London as there was no precedent for an appointed Council to address the monarch on a political issue that was the prerogative of the elected Assembly.

Gordon was now working with the Legislative Council and with some MLAs to engineer the defeat of Smith's government. He succeeded, Smith resigned, and a government favouring Confederation was installed. The new government was, however, on very shaky ground because of the unconstitutional way Gordon had manipulated Smith's defeat. Smith fought back by preparing a resolution demanding Gordon's recall for unconstitutional conduct. The resolution was signed by 22 MLAs, indicating that Smith still enjoyed the support of a majority of MLAs. Gordon then dissolved the Assembly and called a snap election for June 20.

At that point, events outside the province intervened to help decide the outcome. New Brunswick was suddenly threatened by invasion by an Irish political movement known as the Fenians. They were a group of Irish Catholic veterans of the American Civil War who believed that they could advance the cause of Irish independence by attacking British colonies. Around 1,000 of them massed along the St. Croix River in April, 1866. They thought that Irish immigrants in New Brunswick would join them, but there was little local support for their cause. Fear of invasion by this un-disciplined rabble caused panic along the border. The militia was mobilized for months, and troops and ships were sent from Halifax. The Fenian menace evaporated, but the crisis diverted attention from Gordon's manipulation of the Assembly and his questionable call for an election. The threat of invasion was used to argue that Confederation would make the colonies more secure. Perhaps more importantly, many Irish Catholics who had voted against Confederation in 1865 now felt obliged to demonstrate their loyalty to Britain.

Gordon's actions touched off a nasty electoral campaign. Smith attacked Gordon for misusing his authority. Gordon published accounts of his meetings with Smith showing that Smith was discussing the implementation of Confederation. Smith had been inconsistent, and his opposition to Confederation had clearly diminished. Tilley, on the other hand, had never stopped working for Confederation, and he used all his influence with the Sons of Temperance to lock up the Protestant vote. Smith's alternate policies lay in ruins, but Tilley was not certain of victory. He therefore telegraphed Macdonald asking for $40-50,000 for bribes, and Macdonald willingly complied. In response to criticisms of the Quebec Resolutions, Tilley promised that he would fix the problems in the final negotiations in London. Tilley also obtained an increase in the federal subsidy, but it was limited to one decade only.

The result was a complete reversal of the 1865 vote, with the Anti-Confederates reduced from 26 to eight seats. Oddly, the area that stood to gain the most from Confederation voted solidly against it. That was the North Shore where the Acadians might have been expected to vote for a railway and closer relations with Lower Canada. And the counties that stood to gain the most from closer relations with New England delivered the highest majorities for Confederation. The new Assembly met in June 1866. Smith made his arguments once more, but a resolution approving Confederation was approved in July. In August, Tilley and his delegation sailed for London for the final round of negotiations. A few minor changes were made, but Tilley failed to fix the problems as he had promised during the campaign. The British House of Commons approved the British North America Act incorporating essentially the arrangements made in Quebec in the autumn of 1864. On July 1, 1867, New Brunswick became one of the four provinces of the new Dominion of Canada.

Chapter 6

A Canadian Province, 1867-1900

New Brunswickers greeted Canada's first Dominion Day, 1 July 1867, with resignation. Tilley and many of the politicians who had supported Confederation went off to their rewards in the new, larger, more important federal government. A number of minor politicians replaced them, A. R. Wetmore becoming the first Premier of the Canadian province of New Brunswick. He and his new Cabinet got on with the job of administering the diminished role left to the province. They soon discovered that in the debate over terms, it was Smith and not Tilley who had been right about the effects of the arrangement because the subsidy Ottawa now provided was quite inadequate to cover the remaining provincial responsibilities.

Premier Wetmore sent a delegation to Ottawa to request a recalculation of the subsidy. There they ran into the stark realities of Confederation. Central Canadians had effective control of the levers of power, New Brunswick had few MPs and Cabinet ministers, and those politicians now had mixed loyalties to their province and to the new federation. Wetmore's successor, George King, took office in 1870 at the age of 30. King was smart, tough, and determined, and a friend and ally of Leonard Tilley, now federal Minister of Finances. In 1872 they negotiated an increase in New Brunswick's subsidies plus a grant in lieu of the loss of export tariffs on American timber shipped down the St. John. These arrangements temporarily eased the financial problem, but in 1877 the ten-year increase in subsidies that Tilley had negotiated to ease New Brunswick's entrance into Confederation came to an end and the provincial government continued to suffer from serious financial constraints.

Premier King carried out one of the most important reforms in the province's history. Education had been provided by a combination of public (parish) and church schools, both of which received support from the local and provincial governments. In mid-century, pressure mounted for a single, non-denominational, government-run system of schools which would be free for all citizens and teach a common curriculum. In 1871, the King Government introduced The Common Schools Act, which required all property-owners to pay taxes to support a compulsory non-denominational school system. Churches could maintain their own schools, but they would receive no government support.

The proposal aroused extremely strong opposition from the third of the population that was Roman Catholic. Some Anglicans also opposed it, and others opposed the concept of compulsory school taxes. Irish Catholics objected to the loss of government support for their schools. Only one in six Acadian children went to school, so they would be taxed for a service they had not used, and if their children did participate, those schools would facilitate assimilation into the predominantly English-language culture. The Church appealed to the Assembly, but MLAs who had fought for decades to eliminate the privileges of the Church of England were not about to grant special rights to Catholics. The Liberal Government called an election, making a blatant appeal to Protestants by suggesting that the choice was between the Queen and the Pope. That produced a landslide victory of 35 of the 41 seats. The government then began prosecuting Catholics who refused to pay school taxes. The Church took the issue to court and lost. It appealed to the federal government to overturn the legislation, but received little support. It appealed to the Judicial Committee of the Privy Council in London, the highest court in the British Empire, and lost again.

Roman Catholics then resorted to civil disobedience and refused to pay school taxes. The law stated that anyone refusing to pay taxes lost the right to vote for or to be elected to local school boards. Some Protestants in Caraquet took advantage of that law to take over the school board, which touched off a riot since the town was 97% Catholic. Constables came from Bathurst to restore order. They entered a house where some of the Acadian demonstrators had taken refuge, and one constable and one demonstrator were killed. Nine Catholics were charged with killing the constable. Joseph Chaisson was found guilty, but that verdict was overthrown by a superior court because of mistakes made at the trial. The Caraquet Riot had a lasting impact on the Acadians, and has been reflected in literature and songs ever since.

The deadly riots shocked the leaders on both sides and convinced them that a compromise was necessary. Feelings were so strong, however, that it was negotiated in secret, and the main outcome was kept secret. The Catholics accepted that there would be, in effect, only one non-denominational school system. The government agreed that local school boards could rent Catholic schools, and that Catholic teachers would be employed in those schools. Catholic religious orders could teach in those schools, and they could wear their religious garb, but they had to use the common curriculum and common exams. Religion could be taught, but only after classes. Common history texts would be used, but history texts had to be acceptable to Catholics.

It was a reasonable compromise, and the Catholic clergy urged their people to accept it. Property taxes were paid, and Catholics could once more vote for and sit on school boards. But even when Catholics had full control of school boards, those schools were "public" and not "separate" as in Ontario. In effect it was a separate Catholic school system within the allegedly non-denominational provincial system, and as such it worked remarkably well. The problem was settled, and the basis of New Brunswick's education system had been laid. The new common schools soon witnessed significant improvements in the quality of teaching and attendance soon doubled. The compromise marked the beginning of a long tradition in which Protestant and Catholic leaders worked out compromises in private and avoided open clashes between religions. The Common Schools Act was King's greatest achievement, but he also reformed local government. Saint John and some counties had elected municipal governments, but many counties were still administered by magistrates appointed by the provincial government. King's Municipalities Act of 1877 forced all counties to incorporate as municipalities and take direct responsibility for local affairs.

One of the major factors that propelled the province into Confederation was fear for the economic future. In the mid 1870s, New Brunswick's Golden Age peaked with shipbuilding providing 20% of the economic activity in Saint John - only four cities in the British Empire had more ships registered than Saint John. The age of wooden sailing ships was coming to an end, however, and over the next 60 years they were replaced by iron steam ships manufactured elsewhere. One immediate effect was outmigration. In the 1870s, the population of Saint John fell from 41,000 to 39,000, and the city also suffered a disastrous fire in 1877. Overall perhaps 75,000 people migrated elsewhere looking for jobs and a brighter future, and the population aged and became more conservative as the young and ambitious left.

The Intercolonial Railway was finally completed from Halifax to Quebec City in 1876. Because it was 250 miles longer than the route along the St. John Valley, the cost of shipping New Brunswick products to central Canada remained too high to stimulate economic development. In 1869, the Western Extension was finally built from Saint John to Bangor Maine, but without Reciprocity, it did not generate the traffic its supporters had anticipated. The province also pressed ahead with a line running up the St. John Valley towards Edmundston.

After 1876 the economy suffered due to the collapse of the British market for lumber and ships. It then began to improve after the federal government adopted the National Policy in 1879. A global recession in the late 1870's had led to a flood of cheap manufactured goods from the United States which threatened the fragile industries of central Canada. The government responded with a policy of high tariffs designed to exclude foreign goods from the Canadian market. New Brunswick businessmen responded with enthusiasm. Merchants shifted their capital from shipbuilding to textiles, distilling, sugar refining, and a plethora of small industries such as machinery, stoves, carriages, and furniture, most of it centered in southern New Brunswick. In the 1880s, industrial production increased faster in the Maritimes than in central Canada, and Saint John grew faster than the industrial city of Hamilton, Ontario. The town of St. Stephen had the second largest cotton industry in Canada. This was a period of enormous growth of towns in terms of size, complexity, industry, paved streets, sewers, street lights, public transportation, phones, newspapers, the telegraph, and electric street cars.

That growth did not, however, offset the economic stagnation in rural areas. It was also somewhat of a false start. Geography and other obstacles were too strong for the Maritimes to emerge as the industrial heartland of Canada. Central Canadian businessmen did not want competition from the Maritimes, so they bought up competing Maritime industries and closed or rationalized them. New Brunswick banks found it more profitable to invest elsewhere, and were themselves purchased by larger banks outside the province, notably the Bank of New Brunswick which was taken over by the Bank of Nova Scotia. Industrial capacity often became overextended, and capitalists and merchants were sometimes unable to acquire the capital they needed.

Attempting to manage these economic changes and challenges was the somewhat fragile provincial state that had emerged in 1867. The Confederation debate had grouped most politicians into two loose coalitions, the Antis and the Confederationists. The latter won the 1866 election, and remnants of that group remained in power after Confederation. They tended to support the federal Conservatives. The losers from the Confederation debates were mostly Reformers or Liberals, and tended to support the federal Liberal party. A few other MLAs still wanted to vote independently rather than in a disciplined party structure. As a result, while all the governments in the decades after Confederation were mainly Conservative or Liberal, they were also coalitions of MLAs who had switched parties, and three of the first four Premiers had in fact voted against Confederation. Many MLAs had been on both sides of the Confederation debate, and one of them, A. R. Wetmore, commented that at least he had been right half the time.

One of the most dominant of the post-Confederation politicians was Andrew Blair, Premier from 1882 to 1896. He began his career aligned with the federal Conservatives, but changed sides and engineered the collapse of his own government. He then assembled a coalition from both factions and disciplined its MLAs with patronage. Blair was a reformer, and he brought a stronger ideological foundation to his party. He is seen by some as the founder of the modern Liberal Party. One important reform was universal male suffrage, except for Natives. Another was limited prohibition of alcohol. In 1890, he issued the first political platform in the province's history. Perhaps the most important change was the abolition of the appointed Legislative Council in 1891. The Council had vetoed bills passed by the Assembly, and its abolition was a further step down the long road to democratic government. Blair also launched an ambitious program of public works.

The decades after Confederation witnessed a very significant change in the attitudes of Acadians. For a century after the Deportation they had been concerned mainly with survival. Politically they were passive, content to live their lives in their small close-knit communities, working their own farms and supplementing their incomes working for English-speaking merchants in fishing and lumbering. Their proportion of the province's population was increasing as a result of a high birth rate and a reluctance to migrate elsewhere. By 1901, they accounted for 24% of the population and had replaced the Irish as the largest Catholic group. A political awakening was evident when they voted overwhelmingly against Confederation in both the 1865 and 1866 elections. A new elite emerged, based on the Collège St. Joseph which opened in Memramcook in 1864 and Sacré Coeur in Caraquet. The first Acadian newspaper, *Le Moniteur Acadien*, was published in Shediac in 1867, and the more important *L'Evangeline* moved from Nova Scotia to Moncton in 1905

This stirring of nationalism became known as the Acadian Renaissance. As a people they responded to the publication of Henry Wadsworth Longfellow's epic poem *Evangeline* which depicted the suffering of the Deportation. They strongly opposed the Common Schools Act and were rewarded with changes that effectively left them in control of their schools. That Act also brought significant increases in school budgets, and their poor record of illiteracy began to diminish. Acadians organized huge conventions in 1881, 1884, and 1890 to assert their nationalism. They rejected the French Canadian national day of St. John Baptist and selected their own date, the Feast of the Assumption, 15 August. They adopted a flag, a motto, and a national song, and they founded the Société Nationale l'Assomption. Their churches had long been dominated by Irish bishops who favoured the use of English, and Acadians began demanding that more priests be Francophone Acadians. That battle took generations, but in 1910 the first Acadian bishop was consecrated and by the 1930s three of the province's four bishops were Acadian.

Chapter 7

Development, War, and The Roarin' Twenties, 1900-1930

The main railway routes on the southeast and north shores had been completed, plus extensive local networks feeding into them. But the main trunk line along the Saint John to Quebec remained unfinished. The Conservatives under James Kidd Flemming made that the main issue in the 1912 election, which they won with 46 of 48 seats. The federal government was also in the mood to build more transcontinental railways, and the two governments finally completed the line linking Saint John with Quebec City along with the National Transcontinental which ran diagonally across the province. Saint John did not become the Vancouver of the east, however, because central Canada exported and imported by whatever route served its interests, and that meant using the St. Lawrence in summer and Halifax, Saint John, or American ports in winter.

During this period the political system evolved into a party system, with Blair's coalition called Liberal and the MLAs not in that coalition identified as Conservative. The opposition's campaigns usually focused on criticizing the government for corruption or failure to support various projects. Both parties now issued platforms on which all their candidates campaigned, but there was little difference between them. New Brunswickers therefore had a choice in each election between a group of experienced politicians who distributed patronage and a group of opposition MLAs who promised cleaner government and a slightly different allocation of spending. The voters usually returned the experienced team until its level of incompetence and corruption reached such a stage that its own politicians and supporters deserted it. Then, a new coalition took charge, easily winning re-election once or twice. Blair's coalition governed with little difficulty for 25 years, but was finally laid low by a corruption scandal over the building of a railway to the coal fields at Minto.

The outbreak of World War I in August, 1914, was greeted with great enthusiasm. As a British colony, Canada was at war when Britain declared war on Germany. Thousands of men volunteered and marched off to the train stations amidst wildly-cheering crowds. Orders began to flow in for agricultural products, fish, timber, and minerals, and under-utilized factories began to expand their work forces. Soon, the labour surplus turned into a shortage, and then an acute shortage. That demand was met by older men continuing to work, by teenagers, and especially by women taking jobs previously thought to be beyond their capacity.

Enthusiasm for the war lasted for several years but was gradually undermined by a number of factors. One was the growing lists of casualties from the battlefields of Europe, the realization that in every rural area, town, or city block more and more husbands, fathers and sons were never coming back or would return with grievous physical and mental injuries. Another was the way the war was being managed or mismanaged, with enormous profits being made by a few, sometimes from the sale of shoddy products, while the war was financed by inflation which meant that prices rose faster than incomes for most people. By 1916, workers began going on strike for wage increases to catch up to inflation. Acadians came to view the war as an English war, especially as their volunteers were invariably commanded by English-speaking officers. Farmers were expected to produce more and more, but could not buy new machinery or replace sons who had gone off to fight. Corruption and war profiteering were exemplified by the Great New Brunswick Potato Scandal. The Assembly voted money for a huge gift of potatoes for the British people. The contracts went to Conservative farmers some of whom unloaded spoiled potatoes but charged full price if not more. Politicians grew rich and tried unsuccessfully to cover up the scandal when rumours and accusations began to spread.

The War saw the triumph of two old political movements. Women who had lost the vote in 1843 finally regained it in 1919. They could not, however, run for office until 1934. Prohibition also triumphed. Restrictions on the sale of liquor were introduced in the 1880s, but many loopholes were left in the legislation. In wartime it became unpatriotic to use agricultural products for pleasure, and in 1917, New Brunswick passed one of the most draconian prohibition laws in Canada. The United States also introduced strict prohibition laws which led to massive smuggling, a business that involved many fishermen and corrupted the police, courts, and government officials.

It was still impossible to close all the loopholes, and licences were granted for the industrial, spiritual and medical uses of alcohol. Doctors and druggists made fortunes from prescriptions for medicinal brandy. Municipalities discovered that they could supplement their revenue, promote commerce and satisfy consumers' thirst simply by regularly collecting fines from hotels and other establishments for violating the law. Between raids, liquor was dispensed without interference, and the pattern of raids and fines became an established form of regulation and taxation. By the 1920s, it was clear that prohibition was not possible, and the Conservative Government replaced it with a government monopoly on the sale of liquor. Strict limitations were placed on where, when, and how it could be consumed, which ensured that liquor would continue to be sold and consumed illegally.

In economic terms, the war postponed a crisis that had been building since the 1890s. Manufacturing, forestry, fishing and agriculture were all in serious trouble by 1910, but wartime demand produced four years of full employment and high prices. The overall trend-lines remained negative, and the federal government did not address fundamental problems, partly because of New Brunswick's declining influence. Every census revealed that the province's share of the national population had decreased. Its representation in the House of Commons fell from 16 out of 200 MPs in 1867 to 11 out of 235 in 1911. That decline was arrested with a compromise agreement in 1915 that ensured that no province would have fewer MPs than Senators. New Brunswick has been represented in Ottawa by 10 MPs ever since, even though its share of Canada's population has continued to decline. Another weakness in Maritime influence in Ottawa resulted from the fact that Maritimers repeatedly split their votes between government and opposition in Ottawa rather than voting en masse as other regions did, and some regions always supported the same political party. That dissuaded federal parties from competing for Maritime votes. Maritime MPs often concentrated on local rather than provincial or regional issues and interests which further undermined their influence in the federal government.

In manufacturing, the province was at a disadvantage with central Canada because of distance and small local markets. The main underpinning of the New Brunswick economy was the understanding that the Intercolonial Railway would subsidize freight rates to promote economic development in the Maritimes as part of the overall integration of the new Canadian market created by Confederation. That Confederation deal was more of an understanding than a constitutional guarantee, and as such it depended on continued support in the rest of Canada. That support began to decline before World War I as more and more MPs came to question the subsidized freight rates, and in 1912, a 12% rate differential on westbound freight was abolished.

At the same time Ottawa decided to extend the borders of Quebec, Ontario, and Manitoba to Hudson Bay, which represented a huge expansion of their area and resources. The Maritimes argued that this land had been purchased in 1870 with tax money collected in part in the Maritimes, and that if Ottawa was going to give it to three provinces, it should compensate the Maritimes for their share of that federal gift. That argument was rejected, a further indication of the loss of influence at the federal level. Federal spending during World War I also weakened the relative position of the Maritimes because the vast majority of new investment in wartime manufacturing capacity went to central Canada, and when the war ended, the Maritimes faced unemployment and ageing factories.

The end of the war was greeted with little enthusiasm. One form of suffering had come to an end, leaving hundreds of single mothers, young women who would never find husbands, farmers left to work their land alone, and hundreds of wounded men to look after. War's end brought an immediate drop in demand for all the province's products. Women were dismissed from the work force, but that did not create enough jobs for the returning veterans, and unemployment and discontent mounted rapidly. For decades, farmers had been growing more disenchanted with their status as individuals and as a group. Though still the largest sector of the workforce, they had watched their relative status slip, watched rural de-population, watched their villages shrink and their local schools close, and watched their children, relatives, and neighbours move to the towns and cities or leave the province. They began organizing as a political party, and the United Farmers of New Brunswick won seven seats in the election of 1920. Disgruntled workers also entered that election as the Labour party, and won four seats. Neither had much success influencing the government, and they both disappeared as political forces in the election of 1926.

There were, however, some positive developments in the early 1920s. The lumber industry was in dire straits, but American demand for pulp and paper seemed insatiable. There had been no pulp and paper mills before the 1920s, and a number of mills were built especially along the North Shore. Pulp and paper became a major export and created high-paying jobs. Some mills were powered by coal, but the best source of energy was hydro-electricity, and dams were constructed to supply the pulp and paper plants. The best hydro-electric site in the province was Grand Falls where the St. John River plunged 75 feet. The Liberal Government of Peter Veniot was determined to develop that resource for the good of the province, selling the International Paper Company what it needed and using the remainder for commercial, agricultural, and residential use and to support new industry.

Grand Falls power became the main issue in the 1926 election. Veniot had taken over from Premier Walter Foster to become the first Acadian premier. He was an excellent and forceful minister who had laid the basis for the province's modern highway system. He was also an excellent politician, allocating the highways budget to contractors, workers, and suppliers who contributed handsomely to Liberal party coffers, and using patronage to solidify the Liberal's hold on the Acadian vote. The Conservatives, however, were a re-vitalized party under the skilful leadership of John Baxter. He opposed Veniot's policy, and led the Conservatives to a victory with 37 seats to 11. The International Paper Company developed the hydro-electric potential of Grand Falls, and the government lost control of a powerful instrument of economic development.

The continued decline of the economy produced a major movement to force Ottawa to address the region's problems. It was known as the Maritime Rights Movement. The main grievance behind it was the increases to railway freight rates that came about as a result of the integration of the Intercolonial into the newly-nationalized Canadian National Railway or CNR. The CNR immediately raised freight rates in the Maritimes by 40%, and later by over 100%. Maritimers pointed out that the ICR was part of the Confederation deal, but the arguments fell on deaf ears and New Brunswick's exports suffered a drastic decline.

In 1926, Prime Minister Mackenzie King appointed a commission to examine the Maritime economy and recommend solutions. The King government carefully studied its recommendations and calculated the minimum amount of concessions needed to divide, buy off, and weaken political support for Maritime Rights without spending too much money or upsetting other regions of the country. The concessions included a 20% reduction in freight rates, support for Saint John harbour development, and an increase in the federal subsidy of $875,000. In fact, the concessions were far more meager than they appeared as the railways applied the freight rate reductions to fewer commodities and shorter distances than expected, and the subsidies were subject to conditions. Having bragged too quickly of their success, local politicians were in no position to complain once they read the details. The rest of Canada had no stomach for more complaints, and the Maritime Rights Movement withered away.

Chapter 8

Depression and Development, 1930-1960

The slight upturn in the New Brunswick economy in the late 1920s came to a crashing halt as the Great Depression took hold in 1930. Unemployment rose dramatically to around 20%. The value of timber products in the Maritimes fell 75%, and agricultural products by 40%. By 1933, 12% of the population was on relief. Unlike every previous downturn, this time there was little out-migration because the Depression also affected the regions where Maritimers had traditionally moved in search of jobs. The province already had the highest illiteracy and infant mortality rates in Canada, and the Acadians were the poorest group in the province.

As soon as their meager savings were exhausted, the unemployed had no choice but to ask for welfare from the municipalities. Unfortunately local governments were in a very poor position to provide it. Their tax base had always been weak, and they had already borrowed heavily, with the result that fixed interest charges on debt consumed much of their revenue. Property taxes, their main source of revenue, quickly declined because many people simply did not have the money to pay. Interest charges therefore consumed an increasing proportion of municipal budgets, leaving less and less for welfare and other expenses. Within months, a number of municipalities were bordering on bank-ruptcy. Similarly, the province was in a poor position to help the municipalities because its tax base was weak, its tax revenue was falling as people restricted their spending, and it had also borrowed heavily in previous years. In 1930, New Brunswick was devoting 28% of its revenue to interest on its debts, twice as much as the national average. By 1933, interest payments were consuming 55% of the provincial budget.

Municipalities and the province had to reduce spending on services just as demand was sky-rocketing. Funds for hospitals were reduced, and sick people sent home or refused entrance. One category of illness - tuberculosis - was particularly hard hit because people with minor symptoms were not treated even though the disease could best be cured if treated early. Hundreds of New Brunswickers died because of that, while others starved to death. The survivors saw their standard of living fall until diets reached unhealthy levels, and cloth-ing was patched and re-patched or made out of materials such as flour sacks. The worst off were often too embarrassed to send their children to school. Meanwhile, many people with jobs maintained the fictitious belief that people were unemployed because they were lazy. It was therefore made as difficult and demeaning as possible to apply for relief, and welfare workers saw it as their duty to protect budgets rather than look after the needy.

The only source of additional funds was the federal government. It offered to pay one-third of the cost of relief, providing the provinces and municipalities paid the other two-thirds first. The provinces then offered to provide their third to those municipalities that paid their share first. The scheme appeared fair and responsible but was a disaster in practice. The poorest municipalities could not take advantage of it, and the Maritime and Prairies Provinces could take limited advantage so the program was concentrated in Ontario, a perverse transfer of wealth from the poorest provinces to the richest. The 10% of the nation's population that lived in the Maritimes received less than 3% of the federal welfare spending. The federal old age pension program had the same effect. In order to participate, New Brunswick imposed much tighter conditions than those in central Canada and paid only 60% as much. It then reduced relief contributions to municipalities if some of their welfare clients received the new pension.

Other federal policies made conditions worse in New Brunswick, including raising tariffs to protect central Canadian industries and maintaining a high exchange rate for the Canadian dollar which protected industry but harmed resource-exporting provinces. After Mackenzie King's Liberals won the 1935 federal election, their main effort to deal with the Depression was to set up a royal commission to study constitutional issues even though the constitution did not prevent Ottawa from implementing a fair and effective welfare program.

The provincial Conservative Government, which had the misfortune to be re-elected in 1930, grappled with the impossible situation as best it could. One program was to encourage the unemployed to settle on marginal farmland. Families could grow some of their food, cut their own fuel, possibly sell some surplus, have a roof over their heads, and maintain some dignity. Churches strongly supported the program, especially the Acadian clergy which had always encouraged people to settle farther upriver rather than migrate. Hundreds of families took advantage of the program, but they continued to require welfare. Similarly, many unemployed went into fishing because it provided food even if the fall in the price of fish made the business technically uneconomic. Some physical and emotional relief came from the establishment of co-ops and the Antigonish movement, which stressed both individual and community effort through education and co-operation.

By the time of the 1935 election, the Conservatives were thoroughly discredited both federally and provincially, and the provincial party ran for re-election under the name of the premier, L.P.D. Tilley, son of the Tilley who took the province into Confederation. They were easily defeated by the Liberals under Allison Dysart, who gained 24 seats for 43 out of 48. Dysart was the first Catholic to win election as premier, an interesting commentary on the political power wielded by Protestants in a province that was half Catholic. Dysart's election coincided with a slight upturn in the economy and a slight increase in federal funds. He used the additional revenue and further cutbacks to other programs to finance building and paving roads. The program was deliberately aimed at reducing unemployment and stimulating local demand. In the eyes of the government, this program was so successful that direct relief was terminated in 1936, producing a new wave of suffering when the economy deteriorated again in 1937. Dysart's other achievement was some significant reform to the civil service which increased its quality and reduced patronage as the basis for hiring.

The New Brunswick economy was saved by the outbreak of World War II in September 1939 and not by the politicians at any level. By then Canada was an independent country and made its own decision to declare war on Germany. New Brunswickers volunteered by the thousand, partly out of patriotism, perhaps more to escape unemployment. The federal government quickly put the country on a wartime basis, and the demand for forest products and food soon produced a labour shortage. As in World War I, women took the vacant jobs, only this time many of them remained in the work force after the war ended. The war itself scarcely touched the province, except that German submarines disrupted both the fishing industry and the shipping of resources from the province. A construction boom resulted from the building of army bases at Sussex and Edmundston and airfields at Chatham, Moncton, and Saint John, plus anti-submarine defences in Saint John harbour. The war accelerated an old trend towards urbanization as well as a more relaxed view of morality.

Dysart won the 1939 election with 29 seats to 19, a loss of 14 for the Liberals which suggested considerable disenchantment with their stewardship during the Depression. Dysart soon turned the premiership over to John McNair. He was a Rhodes scholar and lawyer, had been the dominant minister since 1935, was a consummate politician, and governed the province almost effortlessly until 1952, winning the 1944 election 36 seats to 12 and the 1948 election 47 to five. Managing New Brunswick during the war was not difficult because Ottawa had effective control of the economy and of government finances, and New Brunswick reverted to the status of a large municipality. One of McNair's achievements was the first major consolidation of rural schools.

The war provided a short-term stimulus to the resource industries, a construction boom, activity in the remaining manufacturing industries such as building small ships, salaries to the enormous number of men and women who joined the armed forces, and much stimulation to local economies from spending by governments, industries, and individuals. It did not, however, lay the basis for long-term economic growth because the federal government concentrated investment in new plants in central Canada and even transferred skilled workers from the Maritimes to those plants. When the war ended, New Brunswick faced a rapid increase in unemployment while the demand for goods was met by the re-fitted industries of Ontario and Quebec.

The remainder of the 1940s was a period of paradoxes. The war had been financed in considerable measure by government borrowing from workers who earned good wages but who could not spend them because of rationing. The end of rationing, the repayment of those bonds, the new federal child allowance payments and universal federal pensions plus pent-up demand dating back to the 1920s produced a surge of spending and prosperity that continued until 1958. The federal government also helped veterans reintegrate. New Brunswickers shared in that boom. Cars, trucks, and tractors replaced horses in transportation and on the farm, new houses sprouted in new suburbs around Saint John, Fredericton, and Moncton and in towns across the province, and for the first time, consumers bought refrigerators, heaters, electric stoves, hot plates, and the TVs which would expand people's horizons while dealing a near-fatal blow to local culture. Provincial governments invested heavily in bringing electricity to farms, a development that revolutionized the lives of a huge section of the population. At the same time, rural life continued to deteriorate as small farms were bought up by the neighbours, rural population declined, small schools were closed, and village merchants went bankrupt as residents drove their shiny new cars down new roads to the new shopping centres in the larger towns.

One particularly bright spot in the economy was the phenomenal rise of businessman K.C. Irving. He was born into a wealthy and powerful business family, part of the English elite that dominated the French-majority Richibucto region. As a young man he bought a service station in Saint John, and then expanded the network of service stations across the province using them as outlets for other products. Rather than buy gasoline from others, he established the largest oil refinery in Canada, which came to dominate the oil business in the Maritimes. He then established his own shipbuilding company, which constructed his own oil tankers along with ships for the Canadian navy. He moved into the forestry business acquiring control of the largest forest reserves in the province, and then built pulp and paper mills. They produced for both the export market and for all the daily newspapers in the province, which he eventually controlled. He was also involved in mining, railways, bus lines, ports, and television. At one time one in seven New Bunswickers worked for his 300 companies, and he was rated as one of the richest people in the world. Provincial governments had to consider his interests when making decisions, and they came into conflict especially after the election of the Robichaud government in 1960.

The province struggled in spite of McNair's brilliant political manoeuvres. It was helped by a number of federal initiatives and programs, including subsidies to housing, the building of the Trans-Canada Highway, federal programs that paid for vocational training, and the construction or expansion of military facilities and bases such as Camp Gagetown. The province also agreed to a continuation of the wartime agreement in which the federal government collected some provincial taxes and returned to the province a lump sum payment. That agreement strengthened the federal government but it also provided New Brunswick with more money than it could have collected on its own. Still, some felt that Maritime MPs failed to make effective demands for meaningful policies from either Liberal or Conservative parties. Maritime governments preferred to complain rather than develop solutions. The federal Liberal leadership contest of 1947 offered the three Liberal Maritime premiers a golden opportunity to obtain federal support but they failed to take advantage of their bargaining position. Issues such as patronage, corruption, government waste, lack of initiatives, and failure to collect taxes left other Canadians with little interest in throwing federal money at Maritime problems.

The 1952 provincial election and the 1957 federal one marked a revolutionary change in New Brunswick history in terms of attitudes towards the responsibilities and role of government for economic development. Views that had held sway since Confederation gave way to attitudes that still prevail. In Fredericton, complaining about the terms of Confederation or their non-fulfillment gave way to taking responsibility for economic development and asking Ottawa to support those initiatives. In Ottawa, defending Confederation as a fair, national deal gave way to accepting that federal policies had indeed distorted economies across the land in favour of central Canada, and that something had to be done to make Confederation fair for all provinces. Co-operation replaced confrontation as the dominant theme of federal-provincial relations. In Ottawa, the change began in the dying days of the federal Liberal regime, but it only became meaningful after the 1957 election.

The Liberals had been in power in both governments since 1935 and were showing signs of old age. McNair introduced a 4% sales tax which was immensely unpopular given the provincial tradition of demanding increased services but refusing to pay for them. The Liberals still had a powerful political machine, a highly effective premier and a near-monopoly on the Acadian vote. The Conservatives had a new leader in Hugh John Flemming, the son of James Kidd Flemming, premier from1912-14. Workers in the hydro-electric industry were threatening to go on strike to obtain the right to unionize, and McNair decided that fighting the unions would overshadow the sales tax and other issues. Flemming convinced the unions to postpone the strike, saving the province from a major dislocation. He then won 36 seats to 16, including seven of the 17 Acadian-majority seats, though the Liberal strength in Acadian regions gave them a higher popular vote.

Flemming then turned his attention to positive initiatives to address the province's economic stagnation. He created the New Brunswick Development Corporation to attract investments by making grants, guaranteeing loans, making joint investments, and improving infrastructure. He helped establish the Atlantic Board of Trade as a research and advisory group, and the Atlantic Provinces Economic Council, APEC, to study issues and propose joint solutions. He was seen as the leader of the Maritime provinces partly because of his efforts to restructure federal subsidies into equalization grants designed to assist poor provinces to maintain services at minimum national levels. By the late 1960s, those grants accounted for 20% of the provincial budget.

High on Flemming's agenda was meeting the increasing demand for electricity with a dam at Beechwood. The price tag of $200 million would make it the largest investment in the province's history. He needed federal support, but the Liberal government refused to help at the same time as it was pouring millions into the St. Lawrence Seaway. Flemming then called meetings of Maritime premiers to develop a united approach to Ottawa. At the 1956 federal Conservative leadership convention, he seconded the nomination of the western Canadian candidate, John Diefenbaker, who would certainly remember the favour when he became Prime Minister the following year. For the first time Maritime politicians succeeded in having a major federal party include their demands, the Atlantic Manifesto, in the national election platform. Flemming then helped elect Conservative MPs, and gains in the Maritimes were crucial to Diefenbaker's defeat of the federal Liberals. Diefenbaker was the first prime minister to agree that the National Policy had, in fact, disadvantaged the Maritimes and that it was up to the federal government to balance that out with programs specifically designed to make the Maritimes equal partners in Confederation. There followed a rash of federal spending, support for the Beechwood dam and other power plants, support for feasibility studies, loans for projects, grants, and especially the formalization of unconditional equalization grants designed to allow Maritime provincial governments to close the gap between the services they provided their citizens and the national average.

In the 1956 provincial election, the Conservatives had gained a seat, and everyone expected Flemming to be re-elected easily in 1960. He had provided excellent and corruption-free administration, had begun serious programs to address the long-standing relative economic decline, and had excellent and profitable relations with Ottawa. The province had seen eight successive surplus budgets along with significant investment in economic development. His government was far from exhausted in terms of new ideas, and in 1960, it reformed social welfare legislation that was decades if not centuries out of date.

The major issue in 1960 election was the new shared cost federal hospital plan, designed to provide hospital services to all New Brunswickers. The question was how the province's 600,000 people were going to pay for it. The government's position was that each family should pay a $50 premium, with government support for those who could not pay. The Liberals argued that the plan should be paid from general revenue, which gave the slightly false impression that it would cost less for New Brunswickers. The Liberals had elected a young Acadian lawyer, Louis Robichaud, to carry the torch in an election they thought Flemming would win. But the hospital premiums and Robichaud's personality, enthusiasm and speaking ability, and his other promises such as attracting more industry and updating the antiquated liquor laws produced an upset. Robichaud won a surprise mandate increasing Liberal seats from 15 to 31 and the share of the popular vote from 46% to 53%. In the 1960s the pace of change would increase dramatically.

Chapter 9

The Robichaud Revolution, 1960-1970

In 1959, the Liberals selected Louis Robichaud as their new leader. From an early age P'tit Louis had aspired to be Premier, and he became an MLA in 1952 at 26. He immediately set out to tour the province, educating himself about it, delivering speeches, building party finances and organization, developing policies, and attracting candidates. In 1960, he became the first Acadian to lead the party to victory. He won two more elections and introduced the most comprehensive reform of New Brunswick in history, possibly the most extensive reform ever carried out in Canada by a single administration. It was costly, though, and Robichaud left the province with high taxes and huge debts.

The new Premier appointed a young, energetic and capable Cabinet that was one half Acadian, the first time Acadians had wielded such power. He reformed the civil service by hiring and promoting more Acadians and by improving education and training. Unionization was allowed, which reduced the number of patronage appointments. By the end of the decade, New Brunswick's civil service was on a par with those of other provinces. It had doubled in size and taken considerable power from Cabinet Ministers, backbench MLAs, local officials, and private institutions such as hospitals.

One of the government's first acts was to abolish the hospital premium. That resulted in increased taxes, just as Flemming had argued, though much of the cost was covered by federal transfer payments. A Royal Commission examined the liquor laws and confirmed what everyone knew - that they could not be enforced and led to drunken driving, disrespect for the law, and wastage of police resources. New laws allowed liquor and beer to be served in licensed restaurants, hotels, taverns, and clubs to anyone over 21 years of age. Dozens of petty restrictions remained, the main effect of which was continued illegal drinking, but the main problems had been addressed, and government revenue increased.

Another of Robichaud's early major achievements was the reform of higher education. Most English students went to the secular, government-supported University of New Brunswick. Those attending the religious-affiliated institutions - St. Thomas, Mount Allison, St. Joseph's, Sacré Coeur and St. Louis - were disadvantaged because they received limited government funding. The Catholic colleges were liberal arts colleges and provided limited opportunities for French-language students. In addition, students from Saint John had to move to Fredericton, a grievance dating back to 1829. In 1963, Robichaud's government created a single university for Acadians, the Université de Moncton, with the existing Francophone colleges affiliated to it. A separate campus of UNB was built in Saint John, and St. Thomas was moved from Miramichi to the Fredericton campus of UNB. All colleges and universities were given provincial grants on a per capita basis, with larger grants for the engineering and science faculties. These changes brought higher education in line with that in other provinces, and the decision to create the Université de Moncton is regarded as a major milestone in Acadian history.

During the election, Robichaud had promised to address the problem of municipal finance. The north eastern counties were poorer than those in the south, so municipalities there had less to spend on education, infrastructure,- and social services even though the needs of the people were greater. Industry preferred to invest in the richer areas where infrastructure was better, local governments were stronger, and the workforce was better trained and educated. That perpetuated poverty, unemployment, underemployment, lack of opportunity, apathy, pessimism, and defeatism in the northeast. The problem was religious and ethnic as well as geographic, because the poorer areas were more Catholic than Protestant, more Francophone than Anglophone, and rural rather than urban.

An initial assessment revealed that the problem was far more serious than previously thought. The demand for better government services was growing, but many people simply could not pay more taxes, and several municipalities were near bankruptcy. There was also an incomprehensible patchwork of different laws, taxes, and services across the province. In 1961, Robichaud appointed Edward Byrne to make a thorough study of the problem. His report proposed revolutionary change to the way the province was governed. It said that the old systems could not be repaired, and the province had to be governed in a completely different way. Municipalities simply could not provide services that were adequate and equitable. The systems of municipal administration, taxation, school boards, and delivery of health and welfare had to be replaced with uniform, province-wide standards funded and administered by Fredericton, and taxation had to be based mainly on people rather than property.

Robichaud and his Cabinet agreed with the overall thrust of Byrne's conclusions, though not with some of the major reforms proposed. They also agreed that the only way to effect the change was to attack all the problems simultaneously because they were all inter-related. That would upset municipal councillors, school and hospital boards, urbanites, Protestants, and Anglophones, but by then Robichaud had won the 1963 election and had at least three years left in his second mandate. The plan depended primarily on federal finances, but it still required a revolutionary change to administration in New Brunswick and major increases to both taxes and debt. The Cabinet decided to fix New Brunswick, and if they lost the next election, then so be it.

The Program of Equal Opportunity involved 130 separate Acts, the central one being the Assessment Act. It replaced the enormous variety and levels of municipal taxes with standard rates that were applied to all types of property everywhere in the province and were administered by the provincial government. Opposition to the reform was immediate and strong. For decades, businesses had played municipalities off against each other by demanding tax concessions before making investments. None had been more successful than K.C. Irving, who paid extremely low taxes on his logging and other businesses across the province. He was outraged that legal contracts that gave him tax privileges for decades into the future were being torn up. On this issue the government was at fault, and it was forced to honour existing tax concessions.

With the assessment problem solved, the government could tackle the other major pieces of the puzzle. The province had a patch-work of local governments including 15 counties and 70 rural districts. County councils were abolished, while town and city administrations were retained. For the local elections the franchise was broadened from property owners to everyone including Natives. The new administrations consisted of two-thirds elected members and one-third appointed, with elections in June of every second year. Their responsibilities were sharply reduced to cover purely local issues such as streets, fire, water, sewage, and recreational facilities, and the province provided their budgets on a per capita basis. They set their own property tax rates, and the province provided additional grants to poorer municipalities.

School administration was next on the agenda, with over 400 hundred local school boards being replaced by 33 school districts, and hundreds of small schools replaced by a smaller number of large ones with broader and more modern facilities. About two-thirds of the new school districts were Anglophone and were found in all parts of the province, while Francophone ones were concentrated on the North shore. Members of school boards resisted, as did those who objected to bussing children long or even short distances, those who correctly saw that losing the local school was a major blow to the survival of small communities and a way of life, and those who agreed that more resources had to be provided but objected to the centralization of decision-making in the Department of Education. Some of the de facto separate Catholic schools were abolished, and common curricula adopted. The province provided standard wages for all teachers, but hiring remained a local responsibility. Consolidation also touched off bitter debates over where the new consolidated schools would be built.

The government took over responsibility for funding health and welfare from local governments, religious orders, and charities. Some of those organizations continued to administer the programs under provincial guidelines and overall supervision, but provincial civil servants took more and more responsibility for health and welfare. Fredericton assumed both the debts and assets of these organizations. Those with debts greatly appreciated that policy; those without probably felt that mismanaged institutions and municipalities were being rewarded at their expense. The confiscation of assets touched off another uproar. Throughout the province, groups and individuals had raised money for their own local and religious institutions, and they bitterly resented seeing the fruits of their work and generosity being pooled for the benefit of others.

The implementation of the Program of Equal Opportunity dominated politics in the mid-60s. Opposition was not violent, but it was virulent. There were numerous stormy meetings, shouting, insults, negative media coverage, and attacks on the program by major organizations such as mayors, municipalities, and some churches. There were threats to Robichaud's life and attacks on his integrity. The government set up committees where people could express their views, views which were overwhelmingly negative. Ministers, MLAs and civil servants launched a massive public relations campaign, distributing literature and calling meetings to explain the programs and allow the critics to vent their anger. Robichaud and others used TV and radio extensively and effectively. To the charge that richer English Protestants were being taxed for the benefit of poorer Acadian Catholics, Robichaud pointed out that the main beneficiaries were rural areas where Protestants were a majority, and the federal government was paying for most of the increased costs. The reforms went through, and in five years New Brunswick made significant progress closing the gap between itself and other Canadian provinces.

Robichaud's attempts to promote economic development were far less successful. Given that forests were the largest resource, pulp and paper mills provided the best opportunity to upgrade exports and create jobs. That goal took on added importance when the South Nelson mill near Chatham burned down, throwing hundreds of men out of work. Long and tortuous negotiations led to an agreement with an Italian company, Cartiere del Timavo, by which it would build a plant that would process annually 150,000 cords of wood into fibre and receive permission to export 100,000 cords of raw pulpwood. To make that amount of cordwood available, the government had to pass a law rescinding leases held by four major companies. Some observers thought this arrangement violated the rules, including John Bates, Chairman of the Forest Development Commission. Timavo then demanded a host of new concessions including cheap power, the right to export twice as many raw logs, and the downgrading of the paper plant to a wood mill that would produce far less value-added and only process 100,000 cords annually.

Robichaud agreed to most of these concessions, even though the province was now taking most of the risks for very little commitment by Timavo. The company then demanded even more concessions, and Robichaud agreed. By then the Conservatives were asking embarrassing questions about the 300% increase in the cost to the province, the delays, the downgrading of the paper mill, the transfer of timber licences, and the special privileges that gave Timavo advantages over other companies. They demanded an enquiry, but instead Robichaud called an election for April 22, 1963.

Pulpwood was the main issue, along with the government's record regarding the liquor laws, its plans for reform, and the usual opposition charges of corruption, waste and incompetence. Robichaud launched a vigorous campaign, defending the record and asking for a mandate to proceed with economic development and reform. The Liberal vote fell from 53% to 51.8%, but they gained one seat to retain a comfortable majority of 32 out of 44. On the pulpwood issue, however, the Conservatives were right. Timavo went on to demand more and more, a desperate and incompetent government ploughed more taxpayers' money into the sinkhole, and the company eventually failed.

Failure also plagued the government's plans for Brunswick Mining and Smelting near Bathurst. With government support it ventured into metal processing, steel manufacturing, chemicals, and fertilizer as well as new mines. Irving had a major interest in this company, and problems between him and the government multiplied. One of Irving's complaints was that some of these projects would duplicate his other facilities. The problems with Irving often wound up in court, where Irving was usually victorious. There were delays and cost-overruns, and while jobs were created, the value of those investments was questionable. Another fiscal fiasco centered on the plan to build an industrial park at Dorchester in the impoverished county of Westmorland. Though it lacked the capacity to evaluate or manage, the government-owned New Brunswick Development Corporation built a fertilizer plant. It then sold it by loaning a private company the money to buy it, but the venture failed, and the government's investment was lost. The park itself cost the government twice as much as estimated, and a floating wharf failed, forcing the companies to ship by rail at a cost the government had to cover.

There were successes in the government's industrial policy, and employment was created in mining, forestry, and the refining and processing of raw materials. The economy was diversified somewhat, and unemployment was reduced in the northeast, but it is doubtful that these investments ever paid a profit in commercial terms. The government was more successful in providing the infrastructure needed by private enterprise. It built the massive Mactaquac hydro-electric dam on the St. John River above Fredericton, a project that involved moving almost 1,000 families and flooding 14,000 acres of land. It also built dams and thermal power plants to provide electricity to the north and northeast parts of the province. The Program of Equal Opportunities and the investments in the economy were immensely expensive. The dramatic increase in federal spending and transfer payments covered part of the bill, but Robichaud more than doubled the sales tax, substantially increased all other taxes and doubled the provincial debt. That legacy would hamstring future governments for decades.

In 1965, the federal government published the preliminary Report on Bilingualism and Biculturalism, an odd title for a study of a nation that had never been bilingual or bicultural. With the population divided roughly 62% Anglophones and 38% Francophones, New Brunswick came closer to that definition than any other province. Robichaud and his government were swept up in the movement to do justice to Canada's Francophone minority, and indeed to suggest that New Brunswick was a model of racial and linguistic fairness and tolerance. Robichaud's own election reflected both the growing influence of the Acadian electorate and a willingness by more Anglophones to support a fairer allocation of resources. Half Robichaud's Cabinet ministers were Acadian, Francophones were gaining ground in the civil service, the establishment of the Université de Moncton was a major achievement, and the Program of Equal Opportunity provided opportunities for the growth of the Acadian middle class.

At federal-provincial meetings on the constitution, Robichaud strongly supported the concept of Canada as a bilingual nation. In terms of French rights, however, all was not well on the home front. In 1966, a huge meeting called Le Ralliement de la Jeunesse Acadienne at Memramcook made it clear that the traditional demands of the old clerical and professional elite were now inadequate. Young Acadians wanted their rights and were not prepared to wait. In addition, they pursued socialist political, economic and social goals, and a nationalism calling for autonomy, provincial status, and possibly even independence.

One flash-point was schools. The government wanted to establish bilingual schools in mixed areas such as Moncton. Anglophones such as Leonard Jones, the Mayor of Moncton, were totally opposed to such "concessions." The government was more successful in creating a Normal School at the Université de Moncton to produce Francophone teachers, but that University was facing more and more problems as Marxist students and unqualified instructors challenged the authorities. Robichaud refused to interfere, drawing the wrath of all sides. The fact was that no matter how fast Robichaud progressed on granting more rights to Francophones, it was never enough for the increasingly vocal militants, and the progress he made was seen by many Anglophones as too fast and perhaps completely unjustified.

In the late 1960s, the language issue boiled over in Moncton where radical students at the University demanded municipal services in French. Students were arrested, and they demanded to be tried in French. That exposed the gap between the government's stated principles and reality, because the courts could not function in French. Robichaud's response was to pass an act in 1969 declaring New Brunswick to be officially bilingual, but it was a statement of principle rather than an action plan.

Politically, Robichaud was one of the province's most successful premiers. He owed that success to his vision, his hard work and dedication, and to his charismatic personality. Implementing the most significant reform program in the province's history took initiative, courage, skill, determination, and flexibility. Fate then smiled on him in 1966 when the Conservatives entrusted their leadership to the radical and flamboyant Charles van Horne whose personal attacks and extravagant promises handed Robichaud his third electoral victory. By 1970, however, Robichaud was worn out from the battles and from family and personal problems. One of many indications of a loss of judgment was that he reassigned rather than dismissed a Cabinet Minister convicted of tax evasion. Robichaud led a dispirited party into an election and actually outpolled the Conservatives 49% to 48%. But New Brunswick elections are often won and lost in the swing seats, and Richard Hatfield took six of them for a victory of 31 out of 58 seats. The Robichaud Revolution, or the Quiet Revolution as Acadians call it, was over.

Chapter 10

The Hatfield Years, 1970-1987

Like Robichaud, Richard Hatfield aspired to be Premier from an early age. His father was an MP who believed that governments had a responsibility to help people. Hatfield inherited that philosophy, a love of travel, and much knowlegde about politics. He had an insatiable curiosity, talked to anyone about anything, loved art galleries and good restaurants, was comfortable with professors and farmers, knew the nightlife from New York to Montreal, listened to modern music, and dressed and acted like a playboy.

Hatfield was elected MLA in 1965 at the age of 34, but none of his Conservative colleagues shared his experiences and few shred his views. He supported Robichaud's Equal Opportunity Program, and would become one of Canada's greatest champions of French rights. In 1969, he won the leadership with only half the caucus supporting him. One year later, he was Premier. He had promised little and he delivered little - the province was tired of revolutionary change and turmoil. He did not purge Liberals from the civil service, and did not change the government's overall policies. One of his few early reforms was replacing multi-member constituencies with single-member ones, a democratic change that reduced the number of safe seats and forced the two parties to compete for votes everywhere.

Hatfield's Cabinet was competent and generally honest. One exception was former leader Charlie van Horne whom Hatfield dismissed for corruption in 1972. Few Acadian Conservatives had won election, but Hatfield put all of them in the Cabinet. The very tough and outspoken Jean Maurice Simard became Minister of Finance and de facto deputy premier. Hatfield took his advice and gave him free rein over politics in the Acadian areas. Hatfield brought in outside experts to make the bureaucracy one of the best provincial administrations in Canada. The Ministry of Finance and the Premier's Office were strengthened so that they could coordinate and control all ministries. Hatfield set overall directions and then let his ministers manage their departments. He rarely attended Cabinet meetings, and he spent little time with ministers let alone MLAs. Conservatives and New Brunswickers soon learned, however, that they had a clever politician at the helm. Three of his new seats were in Moncton, and he immediately approved a school and the expansion of the hospital, meeting demands that the Robichaud administration had ignored.

The government carried on with Robichaud's policy of building schools and hospitals. Hatfield relied on generous federal funding, which continued to flow in part because he cultivated close relations with federal politicians regardless of party. He also introduced an ombudsman, legal aid, access to information, compulsory seat-belts, the reform of family law, conflict-of-interest guidelines, and an advisory council on the Status of Women. It was tradition for new governments to be given at least two terms, and the Conservatives easily won re-election in 1973 gaining two seats for a total of 33 out of 58.

Robichaud's reforms had not brought prosperity to the province, and the northeast remained depressed. Indeed, it was rated as one of the poorest regions in Canada, a status that brought a flood of federal money but no sustained economic development. The closure of the Nigadoo Mine in Bathurst on January 4, 1972, put 300 men out of work and sparked weeks of demonstrations of up to 3,000 people. More and more New Brunswickers found themselves unemployed, and out-migration remained a serious problem. That prompted Hatfield to support Malcolm Bricklin, an American who had designed a new sports car which represented the cutting edge of technology. Hatfield loved sports cars, but he also wanted the province to have an industry that would advertise it as progressive and modern, and he agreed to the fairly modest requests for support. A factory was built, hundreds of workers were hired, and a few cars rolled off the assembly line. Bricklin, however, did not know how to manage a car factory. More and more money was requested and granted. By September 1975, losses were mounting with no end in sight, and the government terminated the project at a loss of $25 million.

That disaster, coupled with falling revenue, inflation, factory closures, cutbacks in federal programs, and delays and cost over-runs of over 300% at the Point Lepreau nuclear power plant, forced Hatfield to break the 1960 promise that he would never raise taxes. He also had to reverse previous tax cuts, reduce health services, and pass increased education costs on to local governments. By 1978 the government was in trouble. The economy was stagnating, and Hatfield's attempts to stimulate it had produced financial and public relations disasters. Like Robichaud, his efforts to promote French rights could not match increasing demands. A series of scandals had dominated the media for years.

The election of October 23, 1978, was the Liberals to lose, and their leader Joseph Daigle did just that. He never seemed to be sure of the issues, one example being promising a rent rebate program which the Conservatives had already implemented. Hatfield took full advantage of that gaffe, calling him a "second-hand rose" for copying existing Conservative programs. One Liberal joked in private that it was better to be a second-hand rose than a faded pansy, but Daigle used the comment in a speech. It was instantly recognized as a major blunder - if Daigle knew what it meant, he had violated the rules of decency, and if he did not, then his knowledge of English was too shaky to be Premier. Hatfield squeaked by with a two seat margin of 30 to 28 seats for the Liberals.

Doug Young then took over the Liberals by forcing Daigle's resignation. That was a violation of tradition in which it was accepted that leaders decided when they would step down. Hatfield exploited it in the election of October 22, 1982. Young also made far too many promises at a time when the economy was too weak to support them. This time, the enormous energy devoted to cultivating the Acadian vote paid off. The Parti Acadien collapsed, and the Conservatives outpolled the Liberals in Acadian regions for the first time ever. Hatfield's fourth consecutive victory, this one with 38 of 58 seats, equalled a record, and he soon became the longest-serving Premier in the province's history.

Throughout the 1970s, language and racial issues dominated politics. Hatfield was determined to give Acadians the rights that fairness and their numbers suggested. There was no French high school in Fredericton, and when one was proposed in 1974, the city refused to make land available. Hatfield made an impassioned speech to city council. It made little impact on the local politicians, but gained Hatfield much favourable comment amongst Acadians. His government then used land from UNB to build the school. He also established a French law school at the University of Moncton, as well as several French technical schools.

Acadians controlled education in the northeast, but there were bilingual schools in mixed French-English areas. Acadians objected to them because they saw them as English schools with some French classrooms. In 1981, a new education bill gave the province 26 English school boards, 15 French boards, and four English boards in which the French had their own sub-units. The Department of Education was also essentially an English institution until 1974 when Hatfield made it a dual department with both English and French deputy ministers.

A significant element in Robichaud's response to Acadian demands had been the 1969 Act declaring New Brunswick a bilingual province. It was a symbolic gesture, and Hatfield postponed giving it substance until the pressure to do so was irresistible. Impatience with slow progress grew as statistics showed that Acadians were no longer growing as a proportion of the overall population, and more and more of them were English-speaking. In 1979, a poll at a huge conference in Edmundston revealed that over half the delegates wanted a separate Acadian province, and some wanted independence. That reflected the influence of the Parti Acadien which was leftist, nationalist, and radical. It had little success electorally, but probably affected the outcome of elections in some constituencies and undoubtedly brough pressure on the government to further Acadian rights and interests.

Finance Minister Simard responded by promising to recognize the rights of the Acadians as one of two founding peoples. A 1980 act acknowledged their right to a distinctive culture, to separate educational and cultural institutions, and committed the government to supporting their development. In 1980, Hatfield also launched a study of the degree to which bilingualism had been implemented. The report confirmed that progress had been limited: while Acadians constituted 28% of the population, they occupied only 14% of the civil service positions in Fredericton. Hatfield ignored the report until 1984 when he announced, against strong advice, that it would be the subject of public hearings. When people focussed on the report they found that it accused Anglophones of bigotry and indifference. That became a self-fulfilling prophesy because angry Anglophones came to the meetings and insulted the commissioners. Instead of providing a blueprint for moving forward, the Report and the meetings roused sufficient public pressure to slow further progress on implementing policies already adopted.

One of the recommendations was for duality in government institutions. The provincial bureaucracy was still an overwhelminglyEnglish institution, and Anglophone civil servants were usually unilingual and resented the designation of positions as bilingual. The attempt to introduce duality into the civil service largely failed, and both linguistic groups remained dissatisfied. Another problem arose when some Anglophones mastered French and were appointed to "bilingual" positions which Acadians thought should be theirs. Sometimes Hatfield's enthusiasm to promote French rights went to impractical lengths. He proposed that the Acadian flag fly over government buildings in addition to the Canadian and New Brunswick flags, but abandoned the idea when Anglophones said that in that case the Union Jack, a fourth flag, would also have to fly.

Throughout this period, language and the constitution were dominant themes of federal politics. Hatfield became a major player, and he strongly endorsed the proposals of Prime Minister Pierre Elliott Trudeau to expand French language rights throughout the country, to entrench them in a new federal constitution, and to transfer the Canadian constitution from British to Canadian jurisdiction. There was strong resistance to all of these proposals, but throughout the process Hatfield supported Trudeau's initiatives. No one doubted his sincerity, and the "national unity" issue was his top priority for years. In New Brunswick and elsewhere he was seen as a statesman and a significant player on the Canadian political stage. He regarded it as a personal triumph when the new Canadian constitution identified New Brunswick as being officially bilingual, the only such province in Canada. Those efforts undoubtedly reinforced his determination to make New Brunswick a model of English-French tolerance, but to outsiders, the New Brunswick of the 1980s was anything but a model of racial and linguistic harmony.

Nor was it a perfect model of good governance. The professionalization of the civil service in the 1960s had eliminated many patronage jobs, and that made fundraising more difficult for the newly-elected Conservatives. The problem was aired at a meeting between Ministers and party officials on August 17, 1971. The party fundraiser, Francis Atkinson, believed that meeting endorsed his plans for collecting money. He arranged for Allan Woodworth to be appointed to the Public Works Department where he could identify the companies that were being selected by professional civil servants for government contracts. Atkinson could then call them and suggest that a contract might be coming their way if a contribution was made to the party.

A number of disgruntled people began complaining of intimidation, and the RCMP launched an investigation. No crime was ever proven, and the Liberals did not make an issue of it because everyone knew that party finances came from contributions by those receiving government contracts. Suddenly, in March, 1977, Robert Higgins, the leader of the Opposition, charged that the RCMP had dropped the investigations at the request of the Minister of Justice, John Baxter. Higgins demanded a full royal commission enquiry, and promised to resign if proven wrong. A long trial revealed that political pressure was not a factor in the RCMP's decision to drop the investigation. The government was exonerated, Higgins resigned, and Baxter successfully sued the CBC for alleging his guilt.

Hatfield then passed legislation to limit contributions to parties, to make contributions transparent, to limit party spending, and to provide public funding for parties. He also reformed the procedures for tendering government contracts and introduced conflict-of-interest laws covering ministers, MLAs and senior civil servants. This legislation was amongst the most advanced in Canada, and supported the perception that Hatfield was personally honest and progressive even if some party officials might be somewhat old-fashioned. Meanwhile, the RCMP continued examining the activities of Atkinson and finally laid nine charges of corruption against him in 1980. All those charges were dropped, but Atkinson was found guilty of paying a civil servant from party funds.

Hatfield himself would soon be tried in the courts of law and public opinion. On September 25, 1984, Queen Elizabeth arrived to participate in the

200th anniversary of the founding of the province. After a day in Fredericton, the royal party was to fly to Moncton for a state dinner. At the airport a routine RCMP search turned up a package in Hatfield's suitcase that looked like marijuana. The media mysteriously became aware that pot had been found. The federal government decided to charge the Premier with possession of drugs. At the trial, which began on January 26, 1985, Hatfield's lawyer argued that the suitcase had been unattended and someone could have planted the drug. The RCMP said the suitcase was under their control all the time, but the Crown could not prove the illegal substance was Hatfield's, and he was found not guilty.

That, however, was only the beginning of his nightmare. The Crown had been prepared to call a witness to testify that Hatfield was no stranger to drugs. Apparently, he had met two university students in 1981, and invited them back to his home where he allegedly offered them pot and cocaine. The next day he took three of them to Montreal where they spent the night in a hotel. Hatfield denied using narcotics, said he was the victim of a smear campaign, and ignored demands for his resignation. Nothing came of these charges either, but everyone involved in the two cases was discredited: the RCMP for their failures and alleged leaks to the press, the federal government for a failed prosecution of a provincial Premier, the Liberals who had lost a leader, the CBC which had lost a lawsuit, and, of course, Richard Hatfield. The issues were so complicated that the RCMP was suspected of both harassing and protecting the Premier.

Evidence mounted that Hatfield was losing his political instincts. During a 1983 visit by Prince Charles and Diana he commented publicly on their marriage, infuriating the British press and prompting some to think he had consumed too much wine. Extravagant travel by his ministers drew increasing criticism, but he could hardly rein them in when his own misuse of the travel budget was so blatant. The economy was growing and unemployment was falling, but those positive trends did not outweigh Hatfield's growing political and personal problems. Hatfield fought well and hard to retain the leadership, and he had solid support from the Acadians and many others in the party. At the 1985 annual party conference, he received standing ovations, and a proposal to establish leadership reviews was defeated. Many delegates probably expected that he would assess the political winds and step down gracefully. But he had never wanted to be anything but Premier, and he soldiered on. In the meantime, the Liberals had reinvented themselves under the young, handsome, and energetic Frank McKenna. In the election of October 13, 1987, Hatfield became the first Premier to lose every seat in the Legislature as the people gave the Liberals 60% of their votes.

Frank McKenna inherited a very different province from that of 1950, because Flemming, Robichaud and Hatfield had modernized the province, revolutionized the way it operated, and made the Acadians true partners if not equal partners for the first time in history. On the other hand, McKenna took over a province that had retained much of its two-hundred year heritage, with its geographic isolation, its dependence on the forestry, its economic challenges, its demographic stability, and its strong Acadian and Loyalist traditions. It still reflected a unique mixture of regional and provincial identities, pro-British sentiment, and Canadian nationalism. No government had ever changed the geographic and demographic bedrocks on which the province was and is based, but the people and their governments had built a province of which their Acadian and Loyalist ancestors would be very proud.

There is no comprehensive, detailed history of New Brunswick. This short history is based mainly on the books identified in the following list. There is much useful information on the web, including the Canadian Dictionary of Biography and Wikipedia. Some of the more important items researched for this project include: Andrew George Blair, Robert Henry Emmerson, Charles Fisher, James Kidd Flemming, John James Fraser, George Luther Hatheway, George Edwin King, James Mitchell, Peter Mitchell, William Pugsley, Sir Sameul Leonard Tilley, Lemuel John Tweedie, and Andrew Wetmore. A great deal of very useful information was contained in the detailed comments of Dr. T.W. Acheson on the first draft of the book.

The main secondary sources include:

Acheson, T.W. *Saint John, The Making of an Urban Community*. Toronto, 1985

Aunger, Edmund. *In Search of Political Stability, a Comparative Study of New Brunswick and Northern Ireland*. Montreal, 1981

Brodie, Janine. *The Political Economy of Canadian Regionalism*. Toronto, 1990

Brown, Keith, and Michael Howlett, eds. *The Provincial State in Canada*. Peterborough, 2001

Conrad, Margaret, and J. Hiller. *Atlantic Canada: A Region in the Making*. Don Mills, 2001

Cormier, Michel and Achille Michaud. *Richard Hatfield*. Fredericton, 1991

Doyle, Arthur T. *The Premiers of New Brunswick*. Fredericton, 1983

Dyck, Rand. *Provincial Politics in Canada*. Scarborough, 1996

Forbes, Ernest and D.A, Muise, eds, *The Atlantic Provinces in Confederation*. Toronto, 1993

Forbes, Ernest. *Challenging the Regional Stereotype*. Fredericton, 1989

Forbes, Ernest. *The Maritime Rights Movement*. Montreal, 1979

Godin, Sylvain and Maurice Basque. *Histoire des Acadiens et des Acadiennes*. Tracadie, 2007

Laxer, James. *The Acadians*. 2006

Machum, Lloyd A.. *A History of Moncton*., Moncton, 1965

McNutt, W.S.. *The Atlantic Provinces*. Toronto, 1965

McNutt, W.S.. *New Brunswick, A History, 1784-1867*. Toronto, 1963

Rawlyk, G. A. ed. *The Atlantic Provinces and the Problem of Confederation*. 1979

Savoie, Donald J. *Pulling Against Gravity*. Montreal, 2001

Soucoup, Dan. *Historic New Brunswick*. 1997

Stanley, Della. *Louis Robichaud: A Decade of Power*. Halifax, 1984

Starr, Richard. *Richard Hatfield*. 1987

Thorburn, Hugh G. *Politics in New Brunswick*. Toronto, 1961

Warkentin, John. *A Regional Geography of Canada*. Scarborough, 2000

Woodward, Calvin. *The History of New Brunswick Provincial Election Campaigns and Platforms, 1866-1974*. 1976

Index